ON THE RIM OF KILAUEA

VOLCANO HOUSE INTERIOR
WATERCOLOR BY JULES TAVERNIER

*Visitors around the fireplace on a chilly afternoon, circa 1886.
The Volcano Art Center is currently located in the 1877 Volcano
House building. The sitting room depicted here has changed
little and is now used as an exhibition space.*

ON THE RIM OF KILAUEA

Excerpts from the Volcano House Register

1865–1955

Edited by Darcy Bevens

HAWAII NATURAL HISTORY ASSOCIATION

To Tom

Hawaii Natural History Association
Hawaii National Park, Hawaii 96718–0074

Copyright © 1992 Hawaii Natural History Association
All rights reserved
Printed in the United States of America

ISBN 0–940295–11–3
LCC 92–85122

Contents

INTRODUCTION

THE VOLCANO HOUSE HOTEL, rebuilt several times, has perched on the edge of Kilauea Caldera since the mid-1800s. For ninety years, the hotel kept a guest register in which visitors could sign their names and write their comments. The Register is now kept under lock and key at the Hawaii Volcanoes National Park headquarters.

This book is a compilation of entries from the ten volumes of the Volcano House Register, covering the years 1865–1955. (The years 1923–1926 and 1940–1945 are excluded because the volumes for those years contain only signatures and dates. Volumes with written comments for those years, if they ever existed, are missing. It is possible that guest registers were kept prior to 1865, but this is not certain.) The entries were carefully chosen from the ten volumes to provide a representative sampling of the different writing styles of each period. The entries are categorized by subject matter into chapters of varying lengths that reflect the proclivities of the hotel guests: most people wrote about the Volcano House, the route they traveled, and the activity of Halemaumau lava lake, so these subjects make up the bulk of the book. Generally, the writing that was most concise was chosen for inclusion in the book.

In this book, editorial comments appear at the beginning of each chapter and throughout the book in the narrow column adjacent to the Register entries. Misspellings have been corrected, and some words or lines have been omitted to reduce the verbosity; however, the flavor of the times has been preserved. Diacritical markings have not been used in Hawaiian words. The use of these markings in the Hawaiian language is very recent and the Register writers, including those who wrote entirely in Hawaiian (such as

· Halemaumau · January · 1917 · *from Rest House on East Bank*

Joseph Nawahi), did not use these marks. To maintain consistency, editorial comments follow the style of the Hawaiian language of the nineteenth century. For ease of scanning, abbreviations have been spelled out and dates have been standardized in the signature blocks. For the chapters on the hotel, transportation, and volcanic activity, the entries are in more or less chronologically placed order to provide a sense of the changes that occurred over the ninety-year period. All the illustrations presented are taken from the Volcano House Register, unless otherwise noted.

Much appreciation goes to Jack Lockwood for his critical reading of the chapter on volcanic activity, and to Kathy English and the Board of Directors of the Hawaii Natural History Association, especially Ellen Kai and Dorothy Barrère (who transcribed and translated the Hawaiian entries) for their suggestions and guidance. The manuscript was greatly improved by the editing of Christina Heliker, Gwen Turner, Jane Takahashi, and Dorothy Foster. A special thanks goes to Thomas Wright, who underwrote many aspects of this project and provided encouragement and editorial help during the course of the work.

85

"Volcano House" May 27th

Arrived here at 6.30 p.m. after a long and tedious ride from Hilo the Volcano apparently very active but being dark and foggy we deemed it advisable not to go down in the crater

James Noble
Kuniakea, Alii
J. Kahooluhi

May 28th 1875

Through the kindness of our host we obtained a guide and made the descent of the Crater. and visited Hale Maumau and Kilauea. which were both very active. in going to the lakes were obliged to cross a lava flow of only about 3 hours previously and were obliged to be constantly moving our feet to keep our shoes from burning. the mass of lava had only cooled to the thickness of a foot or 18in and through innumerable crevices could see the liquid lava. The impression made upon one as he stands at the brink of one of these chasms and views the molten lava struggling, surging boiling, now fiercely beating against the walls of the chasm as if struggling for freedom, now receding to again renew the contest with renewed fury, is beyond the power of words to describe. it must be seen to be appreciated. After watching the freaks of Madame Pele for about an hour and a half we retraced our steps and after again crossing the very recent flow commenced the ascent of the pali. after thirty minutes of pulling and puffing we arrived at the Hotel considerably exhausted having been 5 hours in the Crater

One

THE REGISTER

"I hope these valuable registers will be carefully preserved."

IN 1865, *when the Volcano House was simply an unfurnished grass hut that sheltered people from storms, O. H. Gulick donated a blank guest book to the premises.*

℮

Travelers and passersby are requested by the donor of this book to record their names in it and to note all, or any, volcanic phenomena that may come under their notice during their stay or at the time of their visit. By so doing, this record may become of great value, some years hence, to the scientific world . . .

O. H. Gulick, 2 Feb 1865

We arrived here from Hilo after seven hours ride en route for Kau, encountering some of the annoyances on the road that the foregoing pages speak of. A fog shut the smoking chasm from our view soon after arrival and we diverted ourselves by perusing the preceding pages, which with their numerous contributions from wits, poets and artists we think has served a good purpose though perhaps useless for the purpose indicated in the preface. Many a dreary day must have been spent in its review by this cheerful fire. We are being most hospitably entertained and propose visiting the crater on our return.

E. L. Harvey, Hilo, 12 April 1872

I have found the Volcano House registers extremely interesting; they contain descriptions from good observers, of the appearance of the volcano for more than twenty years; accompanied in a number of cases with

Gulick recognized that the Volcano House was uniquely situated for observing two active volcanoes side by side: Kilauea and Mauna Loa. Kilauea, rising 4078 feet above sea level, contained a large caldera at its summit, about two miles wide by three miles long. At one end of this caldera was Halemaumau Crater, then a molten lava lake perpetually changing form as it overflowed, built cones, rose, and sank. Mauna Loa, 13,680 feet in elevation, also had a summit caldera, called Mokuaweoweo. Although Mauna Loa did not have a permanent lava lake, eruptions were frequent. In addition to activity at the summits, both volcanoes often had flank eruptions along their rift zones.

The Volcano House, then as now, sat on the edge of Kilauea's summit caldera, with a view of both Halemaumau and Mauna Loa. Gulick knew that no one was continuously recording the eruptions and changes of the two volcanoes, for there was no observatory at that time, and scientific parties were few and far between. He proposed a logbook, therefore, as a means of documenting volcanic activity for scientists who would, in years to come, investigate the mysteries of the volcanoes and piece together their eruptive history. Eventually, the Volcano House hut became a small hotel. Over the years, the hotel was expanded and rebuilt several times to accommodate more visitors, and when the pages of a logbook filled up, a new blank register was donated. Although the quality of the original logbooks was quite good, the edges of these books are now frayed from visitors thumbing through the volumes. These irreplaceable volumes are protected in a locked case.

Many visitors, in reading through the old Registers, were critical of what had been written—especially the exaggerations and attempts at humor—and made sarcastic comments accordingly.

diagrams of the lake and its surroundings, which have been made by surveyors or persons skilled in sketching, and show in a most interesting way the changes which have taken place from time to time, within this period. I hope these valuable registers will be carefully preserved.

Charles Nordhoff, 14 May 1893

While here I have read Dana's and Green's excellent works, have copied many of the maps which are found in these registers. Their value is inestimable.

Prof. Elie Charlier, New York City,
12 Dec 1892–3 Jan 1893

Index
Some good
Some mediocre
And much rotten

For the Lord's sake, don't write unless you have something to say and can say it.

[*no signature, no date*]

Two days agreeable stay at the Volcano House and a trip to see Madame Pele's bubbling capers. Thoroughly endorse all that has been said in all the old registers, especially the enthusiastic and imaginative visitors who draw greatly from the ideal.

W. I. Forsythe, Oct 1887

Twenty-seven years of wit and wisdom (some of the former is rather alleged than real) as recorded in the registers of the Volcano House, won't have one half as convincing an effect as the actual sight of Halemaumau.

R. E. Carney, U.S.N., U.S.S. Boston, 6 Jan 1893

If all the wit that here is writ
Were lava, seems to me
A tenth of it would fill the pit
Of yawning Kilauea.

A. Stalker, Ames, Iowa, 7 Jan 1893

In order to compile the collection of entries used in this book, the entire Volcano House Register was transcribed onto computer disks. This made it possible for scientists at the Hawaiian Volcano Observatory to sift through the general entries and pick out those relating to geology, for they recognize the value of these old works just as visiting scientists did in the 1800s.

That fools rush in where angels fear to tread is well known and is nowhere more obvious than at Kilauea. Tourists prove it by their actions at the crater and then writing in the guest books. Roughly speaking there have been about four men born into this world who could have described Kilauea, I mean Virgil, Dante, Milton and Goethe. That the ordinary traveller cannot is abundantly shown by results above and in the other volumes.

B. Dickson, London, 24 Jan 1893

Why everyone should attempt to write on so sublime a work of nature whether they have a gift that way or not is to me a puzzle. As I could not do it justice I will merely say that to me it was the most awe inspiring sight I have ever witnessed—the recollection of it is more deeply impressed on my mind than the shoes I wore were scored by the heated lava over which I walked.

Cicely Adamson, London, 24 Jan 1893

During our stay of three hours, we as a whole were held spellbound at the wonderful and grand sight. It being useless for us to inscribe our individual description of the sight witnessed by us all for the first time, we can only join the hundreds that have recorded their experiences in these "Records," that the visit to this mansion of Madame Pele pays for itself a 1000 times over, and the half can never be told.

Harry C. Hadley, Kenneth Sq., Va., 3–6 Aug 1893

Difficulties arose in transcribing the Register entries, due to the age of the volumes, with their faded ink, torn or missing pages, and spills and smears accumulated over the years, and due to the handwriting styles. Particularly in the earlier volumes, people wrote with ornate flourishes, which are very beautiful but difficult to read. Other writers were simply messy, some to the point of illegibility. In the process of transcribing, many "illegible" words became decipherable because of their context; but since signatures have no context, many of the names presented in this book are only best guesses. It is sincerely hoped that no one will take offense at possible misspellings of the names of their ancestors, but rather, be sympathetic with the transcriber.

Famous persons visited the Volcano House, including Mark Twain, Louis Pasteur, and Queen Liliuokalani.

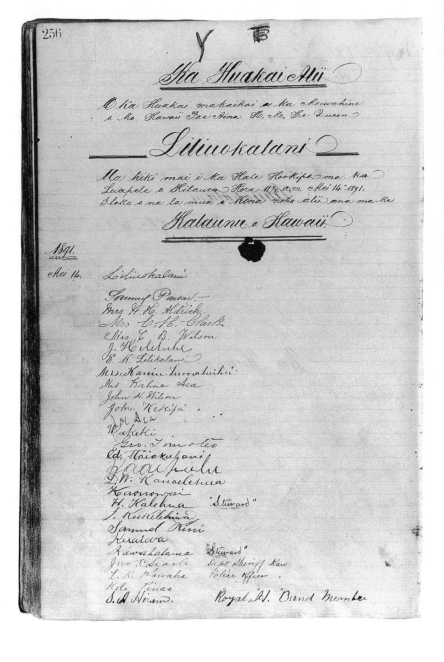

I will not attempt a description of the wonders hereabouts. I have not time and besides it would be superfluous if possible; for none are likely to read this who are not here, and when here they will surely see the wonders for themselves.

S. M. Owens, Minneapolis, Minn., 16 Feb 1905

Upon first reading the many expressions of appreciation by the various visitors, we were impressed with the idea that the proprietors of the Volcano House would be nauseated with this fulsomeness and vowed that we would not add to this nausea, but after a week's stay, and being the constant recipients of kindnesses and attentions, we are impelled to break our vow and with others express our delight.

Mr. and Mrs. H. L. Ross, 4 Nov 1903

Some who thought it was hopeless to attempt to describe the volcano nevertheless couldn't resist penning a few well-worn adjectives such as "awe inspiring" and "grand."

Much of the writing in the Volcano House Register appears to be heartfelt attempts at humor or poetry, flowery exaggerations of the hotel and managers, and overly grand descriptions of Halemaumau, causing the cynical mind to doubt that things were really as marvelous as described. Such was the opinion of Mr. and Mrs. Ross, too—until they experienced the hotel hospitality themselves.

YᵉGAY AND FESTIVE PARTY.
March 23ᵈ 1871.

Two

THE VOLCANO HOUSE

"This is the best hotel in the Kingdom."

IN THE EARLY 1800s *the Volcano House didn't exist. There were few travelers to the volcano in those days—occasional parties of Hawaiians, the Rev. William Ellis in 1823, and Charles Wilkes' expedition in 1841—and the accommodations consisted of grass huts hurriedly thatched together as needed, or older huts hastily repaired. By the time the Volcano House Register was started in 1865, a more permanent open-sided thatched hut, perhaps fourteen by twenty feet in dimension, had been constructed, but it contained no furniture and offered only thin mats on the floor for sleeping.*

After a tedious ride arrived at the hotel if we must term it as such. The Chinaman is very accommodating and tries to make travellers comfortable.

C. L. Smart, 9 June 1865

A party of four arrived here last night, soaking wet, and found the house inhabited by several travellers on their way to Hilo. All that could be done under the circumstances to make us comfortable was attended to, but we should think that this phenomenon of nature would call forth the energies of our people and prepare more enlarged and comfortable accommodations for the travelling public.

O. W. Spencer, 21 Dec 1865

Arrived at this dreary dirty desolate damp place yesterday in company with Mr. Collins Arnold. We visited the crater yesterday afternoon. The weather was quite fair yesterday with the exception of some clouds and it would be quite fair today, if it was not for the clouds and rain.

Chas. W. Marlette, 6 Jan 1866

Having visited Kilauea in the days when the old shed with its open door and hole in the centre, for a fireplace, were all the accommodation for poor weary chilled travellers; how great is our appreciation and admiration of the present delightful dwelling which well deserves the name of hotel. Well may Madame Pele now light up her fires and advertise for visitors since she can receive them with hospitality.

M. A. Chamberlain, Honolulu, 19 July 1866

In 1866, Julius Richardson built an improved hotel of frame, bamboo, and thatch, with a furnished parlor, a fireplace, and two separate sleeping rooms. Visitors who wrote in the Volcano House Register had nothing but praise for the new building, especially those who had stayed previously in the open-sided hut.

M. A. Chamberlain.

I first visited this crater in July 1830. To those who have visited this place in former times nothing need be said in commendation of Messrs. J. S. Richardson and Co. who have converted the sojourn here from a scene of suffering from cold and wet and hunger, into one of comparative comfort.

Gerrit P. Judd, 6 Aug 1866

Arrived here yesterday afternoon, enjoyed a hearty supper after which sat and talked with the polite host, Mr. Porter who is a perfect gentleman and has an excellent way of entertaining visitors and making them feel perfectly at home and comfortable.

George Clark, Honolulu, 20 July 1867

Experienced severe rainstorms during this day, and hailed the sight of this neat little hotel with gratitude. Entering its ever hospitably opened door, the improvements brought since the last visit (of a fine neat fireplace, with its substantial chimney) had power to call forth exclamations of enthusiasm even in a half-frozen and sick traveler. It was indeed a welcome revelation of comfort and good cheer.

Mrs. S. J. Lyman and Miss M. A. Chamberlain,
20 Sept 1867

We cannot but admire, and congratulate ourselves upon the comfortable arrangements of this far away hotel whose chairs, lounges, beds, and not to be forgotten cuisine are blessings so thoroughly enjoyed after so hard a ride in the saddle.

S. C. Powell, 23 June 1868

At this time, John Kaina was the host, although few visitors could spell his name properly. Akona Pake sometimes assisted him.

Tonight the crater looks splendid from the verandah of the House. The enterprising proprietor, J. Kaina, spares neither pains or expense to make things comfortable in this place, and the charges are very reasonable.

Jas. Duncan, Honolulu, 20 March 1869

Today spent six hours in the crater. Madame Pele rather lively. Found the South Lake burning, there being fire in thirteen spots, every appearance of a grand display of nature's fireworks. Received first rate treatment from the gentlemanly steward Mr. John Kane.

Robt. Newcomb, second visit, 19 Aug 1869

The greatest change is in the accommodations now but those who have experienced the discomforts of camping out at Kilauea in old times can appreciate the energy which has been displayed by the proprietors of the new Volcano House.

L. Severance, 16 June 1870

Arrived seven hours from Hilo. Found a great change after six years' absence in a good comfortable hotel and everything desirable for the comfort of the traveller.

H. M. Alexander and J. F. Jackman, 22 July 1870

During a two days stay, have been most comfortably accommodated in this hotel. I cannot speak too highly of the attention paid us by the host Mr. Kain.

Mr. and Mrs. A. F. Houlder, London, England, *no date*

Aprile 21 arrived at the volcana a Drissiling wet Day and nothing to Drink in the house but water a searious Disapointment.

Hamilton McCubbin, Hilo, 21 Aprile 1871

The only serious drawback to the comfort of the hotel is the want of anything more stimulating than tea and coffee.

E.L.C., 24 April 1872

We left Hilo Tuesday morning. Cheered on our arrival with a rousing wood fire and a good hearty dinner. On Saturday morning guided by our attentive host Gilman, visited the domain of Madame Pele, and with reverential awe gazed on the stupendous scene. Language fails to describe what we saw. We found our accommodations so very comfortable, our board so good, and our host, attentive and obliging that we have stayed over today.

signature illegible, 17 Aug 1873

I intend making a visit of eight days at the Volcano House. The climate is healthy, the surrounding country, aside from the crater, sufficiently interesting to induce daily excursions on tolerably good roads, and the house offers that comfort, combined with the attention of the host Mr. Gilman, that may reasonably be expected anywhere. It is rather a matter of surprise with me that the Volcano House has not as yet been selected by excursionists for a longer stay, than the usual sojourn of a day or two. I would recommend to give it a trial for a longer visit.

F. A. Schaefer, fifth visit, 29 Aug 1874

Found the crater quite active. Entertainment at the Volcano House now under the care of Mr. Stackpole very satisfactory.

T. Coan, 21 Oct 1874

Mr. Moore and myself have had a delightful ride around the southerly side of the great amphitheater enclosing the crater, ostensibly to get Pele's hair, at a point about five miles from the hotel. The object in view seemed contemptible compared with the grandeur of the view en route—

The only complaint, in fact, was with respect to the absence of alcohol on the premises.

By 1873, Anthony Gilman had taken over as manager of the Volcano House, with Mr. Kaina and Charles Stackpole as his assistants.

[17]

embracing in the glance of the eye the whole vast theatre of volcano on the left, Mauna Loa on the right, with a breadth of beauty it has nowhere else exhibited, and the snow-capped Mauna Kea to be seen over the right shoulder as you ride. After the dreary monotony of the ride from Hilo to this house and the strange utter absence of all evidence of there being either mountain or volcano within a hundred miles of the rider until one is fairly at the hotel startled by the tremendous black gulf that lies before him. After such an experience in the approach, this ride around to the right makes amends at every point for the majesty that is so wanting in coming in from Hilo. No one who comes here should miss this ride. Nor should travellers imagine that any one or two days will enable them to see what may be seen some days and not others. The writer could not have believed without seeing it, how the show varies from day to day and often from hour to hour, nor how strangely facile it is to be at the verge of these floods of fire and to play with them. I cannot close without expressing the great pleasure we have experienced in finding this most quaint tidy fire-lighted inn and its intelligent keeper Mr. Gilman in a lonely locality that without them would be a dreary nightmare.

Frank J. Scott, 2 Feb 1875

In 1877, William H. Lentz was hired to assist in building an improved hotel. He then took over as proprietor and ran the Volcano House until 1883. When Mr. Lentz was absent, he often left Mr. Robeck in charge. The 1877 building is the present Volcano Art Center.

Arrived from Kau to assist in building new House.

Wm. H. Lentz, 18 July 1877

I visited this volcano forty-five years ago. It was much more active then than now, but the difference is great in regard to the comforts. Then everyone furnished his own larder and blanket and slept on the ground under a poor shanty. Now the accommodations are very comfortable and the table laden with the choicest viands.

Rev. W. P. Alexander, Wailuku, Maui, 9 Oct 1877

Julian Monsarrat

Kapapala Hawaii

The first guest in the New House. Success attend it.

George Morris, South Vallejo, California, 4 Dec 1877

[18]

We arrived July 23rd 1878 a pleasant party of nine, left Hilo at eight o'clock, a pleasant day. Arrived at the Volcano House at five o'clock, felt a little tired, had a most refreshing supper. After supper some went drying their wet things, while others laid down to rest, fatigued after their journey. Others went at cards. Thus the evening passed pleasantly until about eleven o'clock when we all went to bed.

Wednesday morning rose early, had breakfast, then we descended to see the crater, found it very active, returned about twelve o'clock being absent about four hours. Visited the sulphur beds, had lunch, then some of the party went to sleep, others spent the time in cards, some went to visit the strawberry bed, while the rest enjoyed themselves. We expect to leave for Puna in the morning. With much aloha for the Volcano House and the most interesting and obliging host.

Captain Eldarts and party, 24 July 1878

[19]

I arrived here at 3 P.M. this day after a lonesome journey of five hours from the half way house, having met no person on the road and the weather being insufferably hot. But once in sight of the Volcano House, all my gloomy spirits were quickly dispelled, as I beheld the familiar faces who at once went to work to make me comfortable. Was received very courteously by the gentleman in charge (W. Robeck) and we immediately proceeded to take a view of the crater from the verandah, which at that moment Pele was upheaving volumes of lava which was a glorious sight indeed.

William Tregloan, Honolulu, second trip, 1 July 1879

The above named gentlemen before leaving think it but common justice to put on record their high appreciation of the manner in which Mr. Lentz (the manager of the Volcano House) discharges his duties towards his guests. His peculiar manner without apparent effort of meeting the wants of his guests makes them feel that they are not in a strange place, but at home. It is one of the many attractions of this place, and we hope he may long remain here, where he will no doubt draw the same appreciation from others that he has most willingly from us.

James Donnelly, Montreal, Canada, 29 July 1879

The crater appears much the same but not so deep as I remember it, and the action is less. The hotel is an improvement on the small grass home with no residents.

Jon Austin, sixth visit, first in 1850; 16 Sept 1879

Left Hilo at 8 A.M. yesterday. The forenoon was very warm and bright, but soon after leaving the halfway, it began to rain, and ere long it fell in torrents so great we found it difficult to stem the tide; as the road was completely submerged for many miles. Regardless of consequences we plunged forward as rapidly as our trusty steeds could be made to carry us, and reached the Volcano House about 7 P.M., thoroughly soaked through and badly demoralized in general. Were warmly welcomed by Mr. Lentz the gentlemanly manager of the Hotel who soon made us feel quite at home. When after warming and drying before his cheerful fire, we had supper and as the evening was bright and clear were rewarded with a fine illumination from Kilauea. At 8 A.M. we started, with Mr. Roebeck for our guide, and at 10 A.M. reached the crater. The south lake being somewhat active we remained two hours and returned well satisfied with our visit. After indulging in a sulphur bath (which we would recommend to all tourists after visiting the crater) we feel compensated for our trials and tribulations of yesterday. We feel under many obligations to our host for the gentlemanly treatment we have received at his hands as well as to Mr. Robeck our gentlemanly and intelligent guide to the crater.

Sidney Sweet, Dansville, New York, 9 March 1880

We cannot speak too highly of the kindness and hospitality of our host, Mr. W. H. Lentz. His bill of fare might give Delmonico a new wrinkle or two.

L. A. Thurston, 28 June 1880

This is my first trip to the volcano after an absence from the Islands of some eleven years, and there is observed a few marked changes in the general appearance of things. In the first place I might mention the fact of the road from Hilo to here being much longer than it formerly was; it took me some ten hours to make the thirty miles. Everything you know grows with time. The most agreeable change was to be found right in this house and its host. Mr. Lentz—generally known as "Bill"—is a grand good entertainer and keeps everything about the premises in very first-class order, and this seems to be the verdict of all.

O. T. Shipman, 28 April 1881

Slightly damp on arriving. Agreeably surprised at the accommodation. Roused at 2 A.M. and were fortunate in seeing a magnificent flow of lava—probably from the South Lake.

Lieut. J. E. Goodrich, 20 Sept 1881

Visited the lakes today starting at 9:20 A.M. and got back at 12:30 P.M. I shall try for Hilo in the morning first putting myself outside of one of Lentz's renowned breakfasts.

A. E. Hecht, San Francisco, Cal., 10 Nov 1881

Shall carry away pleasant recollections of our host Lentz, equally famous for his geniality and cuisine. Have borrowed Mr. Lentz's canoe, in which to make the passage to Hilo tomorrow.

Joseph H. Skinner, Sydney, New South Wales, *no date*

I cannot leave without a word of thanks to our host Mr. W. H. Lentz whose only idea has been to make us comfortable in which he succeeded perfectly.

E. Asheley Phillips, England, 6–9 Jan 1882

With best wishes for Mr. Lentz, the kind and attentive proprietor of the Volcano House, and for Mr. Robeck the intelligent and skillful guide, who has contributed so much to render pleasant and instructive my visit to the scenes of this famous mountain.

Fred W. M. Holliday, Winchester, Virginia, 23 April 1882

This is the best hotel in the Kingdom.

J. M. Nelson, 10 June 1882

The management of the Volcano House is second to none in the kingdom, and could be well copied by a house in Honolulu of far greater pretensions. I reckon that all who come here will be pleased, the combination of a cool atmosphere, a genial host, a table thoroughly supplied with various delicacies which could not be expected here and last though not least good beds and warm fires make it a place where one would like to remain for a week.

signature illegible, Louisiana, 6 Dec 1882

I fully endorse the remarks of Mr. Webbe on page 469—the Hawaiian Hotel in Honolulu would do well to come up here for a lesson or two and I would recommend Mr. Lentz to publish a book "How to make guests at home" and especially send one to the above named proprietor.

Wm. Reynold, San Frisco, Cal. and Leicester, Engl., 17/20 Feb 1883

In 1883, William Lentz left, and O. T. Shipman took over the Volcano House, managing the hotel until 1885. Guests were as pleased with the new manager as they had been with the old.

Arrived at VH July 1877
Left   "   April 1883

Wm. H. Lentz, 25 and 26 April 1883

Second visit. Considerable change in the form of walls of crater within the year. The present host is no less hospitable and pleasant than the former, but makes his guests comfortable.

L. W. Simpson, Christiansburg, Va., 16 May 1883

After travelling over half the civilized and uncivilized world I can congratulate Mr. Shipman on having a house of accommodation that is not surpassed or equalled for its excellence (excepting pens) by any other that I have visited at such a distance from any town.

Tom Southwick, Hull, Eng., 20 Oct 1884

After dinner we went down to the crater and gazed upon the fiery furies of Madame Pele and realized that the word paintings of accomplished masters nor the brush of artist had never yet adequately portrayed this indescribable and hellish chaos—this mundane hades. The following day H. had a birthday and mine host Shipman having been advised a week ahead gave us the following menu: White snail soup, Pelehu o Kuahini, bananas a la Hawaiian, mountain mutton, kalo and petit pois, laulau moa, poi, uki salad, pudding ala hopu, ohelloo, wild strawberries, Kona coffee noir, mountain dew, Zinfandel, Pommery Sev., Cognac. H. declared after this that he should never survive another birthday.

Henry T. Poor, 7 July 1884

THE GREATEST SHOW ON EARTH
The Great Craters
OF HALE-MAU-MAU and KALEAU!
Billows of liquid fire!
Waves of molten lava!!
Fiery fountains!!!
UNPARALLELED
PYROTECHNIC DISPLAYS!!!!
Day and Night

Goddess Pele, Proprietress

Geo. D. Dorrin, Berkeley, Cal., 19–21 April, 1884

Of course, as everyone knew, no matter how wonderful the hotel and hosts were, the *real* attraction was Madame Pele.

[23]

In 1885, the Volcano House came under new ownership, and everyone was delighted with the manager, John Maby.

The Volcano House passed into the hands of the "Wilder Steamship Company" June 20th, 1885, with J. H. Maby as manager.

no signature, 20 June 1885

Can safely recommend Mr. J. H. Maby as the most kind, obliging and attentive host that it has been my good fortune to fall in with; and can safely say that the few days spent at his house have been the most enjoyable of any I have spent during my visit to the Hawaiian Islands.

H. C. Roberts, Walsall, England, 16 July 1885

Mr. Maby is the right man in the right place, and if one thing is needed more than another in an establishment of this kind, it is an obliging, courteous and good-hearted man, such as we have proved Mr. Maby to be. I think I may fairly say that the "Wilder Steamship Company" may congratulate themselves upon having secured the services of such a thoroughly practical and good all round man.

In crossing the lava of Kilauea to Halemaumau, I'd strongly advise both Ladies and Gentlemen to wear leggings and strong thick soled boots, and each person to carry a lantern if they cross after dark. I would strongly advise Ladies not to cross after dark—but rather arrange, if possible, to remain at Halemaumau all night, which can easily be accomplished, providing they take blankets with them. Our two visits to the two lakes have been very gratifying—the most sublime and awfully grand sight in the world.

Merton and Annie Cotes, 21 July 1885

Hoping that the new owner would make physical improvements to the Volcano House, D. H. Hitchcock penned some constructive criticism.

Now as to the "new departure" in the Volcano House, by Wilder Steamship Co. The whole premises need repairs badly. A little whitewash and paint would vastly add to its appearance. Better accommodations for horses and animals need to be made. Oats do not want to be fed out in bottomless boxes, but good stable room is wanted. Good covered iron tanks are needed instead of the large open tank now half filled. The roof of the building ought to be of corrugated iron, so that the water can be clear and clean instead of running off the mossy roof, carrying with it dirt and moss into the tank. And generally the whole place ought to be kept scrupulously clean and neat. Mr. Maby is trying to remedy some of these things, but a great deal remains to be done, to make this a popular resort. There is no reason why the table should not be better supplied. Fresh milk, and butter made on the place ought to be supplied in abundance.

A good supply of beef, mutton, and fowls ought to be constantly on hand. Beef will keep well up here, protected from the flies, for a week. There is no reason why a first class table should not be furnished for the prices charged. No one feels like growling at a charge if he thinks he is served as well as he might be. I am not saying this to find fault with our kind host, but only to stir up the owners of this place to do more for the traveling public than they are now doing. Have enjoyed my stay of two days up here very much.

D. H. Hitchcock, 23 Aug 1885

Arrived here Friday 1 P.M. from Hilo via Puna. While at Kahaualea, stopped at the mail carrier's house and had first class treatment. While there had a bath in a splendid pool of water a short distance from the Government Road, Makai, in a grove of cocoanuts. Also went down a mile and a half to visit the famous heiau of "Wahaula," where human sacrifices were frequently made. I have, from measurements roughly taken, drawn a sketch of the heiau in the Volcano Sketchbook. It is well worth a while to go out of one's way to see this relic of the Ancient Hawaiian Mythology. Kaahumanu was the first woman to enter the sacred precincts after the kapu was broken.

The Wilder Steamship company have certainly done a great deal of good work on the Keauhou Road and the Volcano House itself with its clean coat of whitewash. Fences all up, gates in good order, flowerbeds etc. show that the manager of this hostelry has not been idle during the year last past.

D. H. Hitchcock, 29 Aug 1886

His wish came true, as indicated in his reappraisal a year later.

The burning lake and Mr. Maby's chicken pot pie can't be beaten.
Abe L. Brown, San Francisco, 19 Feb 1886

Meanwhile, praise for Mr. Maby and the Volcano House continued.

I came to the Volcano House for the benefit of my health and must say that the climate, the comfortable and clean beds, the good well prepared food, the sulphur baths and the kind treatment I have received at the hands of Mr. and Mrs. Maby have made me feel like a new man. I can not help but feel surprised that people from Honolulu especially and the different islands also don't come here to the Volcano House when they need a rest, because everything that can be done for them is certainly done by the manager and his good lady. Only regret that Madame Pele was not at home when we called on her, but the grand and awe inspiring sights we saw repaid us quite for any hardships we had to go through, if any, on our return home. The weather during the time I have been here has not been such as one would call favorable but the open hearted welcome which I invariably received after a tramp in the surrounding woods has always cheered me up.

John G. Eckardt, 24 Jan 1887

Having spent a month here I can thoroughly recommend it as the most comfortable hotel, not excepting the Royal Hawaiian, in the Islands. As every traveller knows, a hotel, to be comfortable, depends on the manager and that is the secret here, excellently managed as it is by my kind host and his no less agreeable wife. I have taken a number of excellent photographs of the crater and I here must express my thanks to Mr. Maby for accompanying me and giving his valuable may I say professional assistance.

Scott B. Wilson, Naturalist, *no date*

The volcano fountains very fine, especially on Tuesday. The natural features of the district are full of interest. The host very attentive and friendly. I wish the S.S. companies would facilitate travellers using them both for the trip if they desire a longer stay. The present arrangements make such a plan expensive.

Edward Clifford, London, 14 Jan 1889

Indeed, the Volcano House and its surroundings were so captivating that many visitors began complaining that the Steamship Company's transportation schedule ought to be changed to allow a longer stay at the Volcano House; some visitors even discarded their return tickets so as to remain longer.

The manager's concern for the safety of his guests was well appreciated.

Being so satisfied with our quarters, we abandoned the return portion of our tickets by W. G. Hall and intend to remain here for three days longer and return via Hilo to Honolulu. May Mr. and Mrs. Maby long be spared to continue their genial hospitality and give similar comforts to future visitors.

Jas. W. Bruce, 16 Feb 1889

We the above party of eleven left for the crater at half past three this afternoon. During the time we were away several shocks of earthquake (twelve in number) from 6:12 to 8:45 took place and Mr. Maby felt very much alarmed for our safety. He sent out guides to look for us.

Mr. and Mrs. Roebuck, England, 4 Nov 1889

March 31st 1891 the last day of the Wilder Steam Ship Co. as owners of

the Volcano House. April 1st the place has passed under the management of the new Volcano House Co. with W. R. Castle as President.

no signature, no date

First load of lumber for the new Volcano House arrived here at 1 P.M. Five hours from the Half Way House.

E. N. Hitchcock, 11 May 1891

For the information of tourists as to the time of building New Hotel, I make this record. I arrived here June 25th and commenced work June 29th. Workmen's names: J. H. Craig, Foreman, Al Gilbert, A. Anderson, Wm. Lewis, [*the list continues*].

Geo. A. Howard, 29 June 1891

In 1891, the Wilder Steamship Company relinquished ownership to the Volcano House Company. The new owners immediately set about building a new and larger hotel, complete with a tower, under the direction of George A. Howard. The old 1877 Volcano House remained as an extension attached to the new building. It was used as a parlor or social hall and included a billiard table which occasionally doubled as a bed.

The new manager of the Volcano House was Peter Lee, who had previously managed other hotels, one in Punaluu and the Halfway House in Kau. He ran the Volcano House until 1898.

I am free to say that I believe that the Volcano House is a first class place to stay. I wish I was so situated that I could remain several weeks, to explore this wonderful country. Mine host Mr. Lee is a capital landlord and did his utmost to please his guests.

signature illegible, 1 July 1891

At this point we the above tourists found the New Kilauea Volcano House Company's large new hotel building progressing in a most substantial manner and notwithstanding the large number of mechanics to be boarded we find that our host Mr. Peter Lee is a most genial and perfect caterer.

H. C. Runger and party, Seneca Falls, N.Y., 1 Aug 1891

Commenced work on New Hotel June 30, 1891. Finished the Hotel buildings October 9, 1891. The number of men employed would average about fifteen.

Geo. A. Howard, Los Angeles, Cal., 10 Oct 1891

For the fifth day since leaving Hilo, the weather has been perfect. Life at this altitude seems full of a charm unknown 4000 feet below at sea level.

S. E. Bishop, 11 April 1892

S. E. Bishop,

I find in the accommodations, the conveniences and comforts now abundant near Madam's domain as great a change as in her Halls. Instead of the little City (as it would be called in western U.S.A.) now here, with its elegant, roomy, well furnished Hotel and Stables, its well stocked larder, its most amiable, obliging & competent Landlord, Lady, and trained servants, ample means for securing an abundant supply of the best of water for man and beast—fresh meat, milk, eggs, butter, and poultry—hot, cold and steam sulphur baths, furnished by Madam P. herself, there was not an ounce of either meat or drink to be had—not an inhabitant or inhabited dwelling within miles of the Crater, and the only shelter for the weary Pilgrim, however wet, cold and hungry he arrived, there was literally nothing to recuperate the physical man, unless brot with him, and nothing to shelter his aching bones except a straw-covered shed with open front and end, on the brink of the Crater.

J. H. Wood, 28 April 1892

The changes here at the Volcano House, in twenty years, are as great and surprising as those in the crater itself. On my first visit, in 1873, we found here a very small house and very poor accommodation, though a very willing and obliging man in charge. We were obliged to climb and scramble down by a very poor path, to the lava plain and across it there was no trail at all, but we followed our guide, climbing over lava hills and blocks.

Now we found here a commodious and admirably kept hotel, with excellent service and as good food as one gets in Honolulu—better one of our party says. The sulphur baths so comforting after the journey are well arranged and fitted; and a broad and well smoothed trail almost worthy to be called a road leads down into the great crater, and over the lava plain, to the lake. In front of the lake a lava house has been built, which gives shelter for a large party against the cool or sometimes cold wind, and enables one to watch the fiery display conveniently. One now goes down on horseback—with safety to the poorest riders, and the horses kept here are gentle and sure-footed. I find it is now usual for visitors to go down to the lake in the evening, the display being of course most brilliant and effective at night, but I advise all who come here to go down also by day, so as to examine the great lava plain, as well as the fiery lake. The charges at the Volcano House are so moderate for horses and guides that the visitor may spend much of his time in the crater, and see it also by a drive or ride about its upper walls. The air is fresh and delightful at this height, and the climate excellent.

I suggest to visitors to spend a night, I mean a whole night, in the crater house; which can be done without discomfort, even by ladies, if they will secure a mattress and blankets to be brought there from the Volcano House, with a lunch for the middle of the night. The evening one spends there is too short; and every one of our party wished to spend a whole night in front of the lake.

To watch, by the hour or day the changes in the behavior of the fiery lake, is the most fascinating spectacle I know of in the world. To be able to do this and return when tired, to an excellent meal or comfortable room and bed is certainly as pleasant as it was unexpected by me.

Charles Nordhoff, 14 May 1893

Every so often, a writer would recall the old days and contrast them with the splendor of the new hotel.

The genial manager of the hotel was at the front door to receive us with open arms; in half an hour's time we were donned in dry clothes and seated at a cheerful and bountiful table. The following day (Thursday) at 4:30 P.M. we started for one of the "Greatest Wonders of this Globe," reaching our destination after a fifty-minute walk over the new and excellent trail made by Lee himself, for which much credit is deserved. During our stay of three hours, we as a whole were held spellbound at the wonderful and grand sight. Before coming to a close would drop a line in favor of the "Ohelo," so delicious with milk and sugar, better still in a shortcake. All that has been said in reference to the manager is not exaggerated in the least, he is all that has and can be said, his whole attention and study, is for his guests.

Harry C. Hadley, Kenneth Sq., Va., 3–6 Aug 1893

Mr. Lee continued to receive compliments in the Register, although visitors occasionally found it necessary to outwit him.

Four A.M. visited crater. Twenty-eight fountains were playing. Combined light from lanterns and crater formed an awe inspiring sight. Visitors are strongly recommended to visit Madame Pele by night. Mr. Lee's opposition may be overcome by strategy. Hide lamps and sticks in your beds.

no signature, 2 April 1894

Visitors also praised other members of the staff.

Mr. Lee, the host, is genial, kind, and obliging. This has often been said before but I am afraid that not enough has been said for Ah Hee. Hee seems to be the ruling spirit among the guests. At table we find him smilingly passing the ohelo berries. When we go to our rooms Ah Hee is making up the beds. When in need of a sulphur bath Hee turns the steam on; towels, hot or cold water, fires and all sorts of things are at your disposal if you call on Ah Hee. Long may he live.

Margaret Roche, Honolulu, 8 Aug 1894

I saw Madame Pele this night, with an awestruck heart. I praise the Lord for the marvel of one of his many wondrous works. Oh travellers, do not complain of discomfort. The price is reasonable for the meeting with Pele. Above is the beautiful crater, and below, this room. I give my highest regards to Mr. Peter Lee, the Manager of this Hotel. Adieu, Madame Pele. [*Translated from Hawaiian.*]

J. W. Waipuilani, North Kona, Hawaii, 14 April 1895

Should I ever be fortunate enough to find my way hither again it would be to see not the greatest volcano on earth but the "greatest landlord on earth." Mr. Peter Lee and his brother Mr. Martin Lee both make it so nice and comfortable for all their visitors. I have been here about twelve days and have found everything highly enjoyable.

William Ross, Honolulu, 8 March 1895

Altho' the volcano is quiescent just now, no one with a love for beauty can regret the trip here. For many miles the stage road passes thro' a splendid wilderness of tropical growth, among which the multitudinous variety of ferns easily usurps first place. From the aerial bird's nest fern and towering tree-fern to the delicate woodwardias and ebony-stemmed maidenhairs, the observer notices dozens of unknown, dainty fronds, sheltering their richness of colors beneath huge boulders of volcanic ancestry or drooping banana leaves. It is wonderful to see such luxuriance hiding the scarce-cold evidences of the life-destroying element of fire.

Harold S. Channing, Pasadena, Calif., 23 March 1897

The impressive scenery is well set; all corresponds: rare pulu ferns, sandalwood trees, yawning chasms, and crystallized sulphur openings—with the ever rising vapors, and ever changing surface of black lava. One who has never stopped in the rush of life before, can not fail to pause here in wonder at the majesty—the sublimity of the spot.

Mrs. Henry Stockbridge, Baltimore, Maryland,
17 May 1897

While you are at the Volcano House, do not fail to see the sunrise. If you are not good at getting up in the morning, stay up all night to see it. It is worth it. The glistening white dew upon the grass at your feet, the dark, tremendous outline of Mauna Loa against the rosy sky in the west, the sunrise glow in the east, before you the black crater dotted with flecks of white cloud from the steam holes—all around you the mysterious, divine stillness of the dawn forms a picture to carry in memory the rest of your days.

Eliza A. Conner, 17 Dec 1898

The drive from Hilo to Volcano House was simply grand, words cannot be found to convey to a second person the beauty of the country. Tourists must come and see for themselves. Our reception at Volcano House from

Even when the volcano was not erupting, people were delighted with the hotel and its tranquil surroundings.

In 1898, Fred Waldron took over as manager, a position he held for about two years.

Mrs. and Mr. Waldron was of the kindest and they seemed to try and excel each other in making their visitors comfortable, also giving all the necessary information for their guidance in sight seeing.

C. G. Conradi, Commanding S.S. "Garonne"
of Liverpool, Dec 1898

The Volcano House under the management of Mr. Waldron is worthy of a visit even if Madame Pele is only doing her cooking with gas instead of fire.

John M. Vivas, 6 Aug 1899

Arrived here from Makaweli, Kauai, Sept 1, 1899 and after spending a few weeks in this cool climate returned invigorated and much satisfied with our Host and Hostess who did everything in their power to make our stay here pleasant and agreeable. The journey from Hilo is now easy and delightful. The new Volcano House is also a great improvement upon the old one and contrasts favorably with former accommodations.

H. Morrison, *no date*

The ride from Hilo to Volcano House is enough to repay trip. We came here intending to stay but a few days, but we found the place so attractive, the hostess and her husband so kind and hospitable that we decided to stay as long as possible, not wishing to return to Hilo after our stay here.

Jas. Sels, Oakland, Cal., 16 July 1900

The Waldrons were extremely concerned for their guests, just as previous managers had been, going out of their way to ensure both that the visitors were safe and that they were provided with every opportunity to see eruptions.

We made a trip to the crater by day and one by night—both of which were interesting. At night the cracks burned a fiery red and we amused ourselves cooking eggs, baking bananas and burning sticks. We went into the hot cone and felt the heat of 130 degrees, and charmed by the interesting wonders and moonlight, almost forgot to come back—so, much to our surprise when we were coming through the moonlit forest of ferns we met a search party—fearful that the edge had caved in and that we were no more. The relief of the host and hostess (Mr. and Mrs. Waldron) at our return, was shown in a very charming midnight repast and a hot crackling wood fire.

Mrs. Edith Maling, 19 June 1902

The above party left this a.m. very much disgusted at not seeing the volcano active. At 4 P.M. Mr. Waldron kindly telephoned Mr. J. L.

Robertson at his home in Olaa—and we all returned—for we were told that the lake had broken out again. To say that we were surprised would be putting it mildly—and the sight we saw was simply magnificent, sublime, grand; words cannot describe the action of the crater.

T. A. Hays, 14 Sept 1902

We saw a small fire in the bottom of an awe-inspiring pit 800 feet lower than the place where we stood.

This morning all was changed—at four o'clock our genial host—Mr. Waldron—aroused us to behold a bright sky in the direction of the crater and we could easily see that something extraordinary was taking place. Quickly, the horses were saddled. After reaching the corral and tying our horses, we commenced a run to the edge of Halemaumau and there saw what our words are too poor to attempt to describe. The whole bottom of the immense crater was one lake of fire, with a great fountain off to one side, pouring out a tremendous stream of molten lava which had already filled the pit to the extent of some forty feet during the course of the night.

Gazing on this wonderful sight, one cannot help but realize the poverty of paintings, compared with the volcano itself, in color, the poverty of words in description and we are inspired with the most exalted ideas of the magnitude of the works of the Divine Creator.

It is with deep regret that we leave this spot, which is so beautiful, so grand, so magnificent—in short indescribable.

Mrs. M. E. Clark, Portland, Maine, 9 Nov 1902

The time has come when the U.S. Government might well reserve the whole region from Mokuaweoweo to the sea, at Honolulu in Puna, a long narrow strip to include Kilauea and the line of pit craters to the sea; a comparatively worthless tract of country commercially. It should also include the koa tree molds at Kuapuawela, where a forest of giant trees were surrounded by a deep flow.

W. R. Castle, 21 Jan 1903

In the early 1900s, people began to suggest the need to establish a national park that would encompass the area of the volcano.

William R. Castle

After Mr. Waldron left, St. Clair Bid-good became manager until 1904.

No trip to the Paradise of the Pacific is complete without a visit to Kilauea. Any unpleasant memories of the sea are forgotten as you behold the wondrous beauty of this mysterious place. Honolulu is interesting, at Hilo you catch a glimpse of real native life, but at the Volcano you receive a lasting impression of the wonderful works of nature. The road from Hilo winds through the most luxuriant tropical vegetation; the banana, palm, and tree fern form a canopy of beauty which makes you think you are in fairyland, but however much you may have enjoyed these you cannot but be impressed with the awful grandeur of the volcano. One stands in awe as he beholds the mighty forces of nature at work and realizes more fully than ever before the wonderful things that God hath wrought. We suggest as long a stay as possible as the grandeur of the place grows upon you. Our visit of five days was all too short.

No mention of Kilauea would be complete without including our good host Mr. St. Clair Bidgood, Manager of the Volcano House, who left nothing undone which could add to our enjoyment.

Waterhouse party, 11 March 1903

For snow capped mountain peaks, rugged rocks, fiery pits, bracing air, complete cuisine, good service and the most congenial of hosts, visit the Volcano House.

C. K. Maguire, Manila P.I., 5 July 1904

Kilauea is one of those rare spots where Nature improves on acquaintance. At first she seems harsh and forbidding and impresses one with the awful grandeur of her works, but with a more intimate acquaintance her spirit mellows and her bearing becomes more friendly, congenial, sympathetic and always interesting and entertaining. We have now been here for six weeks, and we are indeed loath to leave. The ever changing condition of Kilauea, the numerous craters in this vicinity, the forests, the caves and the mountains have been a source of ever increasing interest to us, and we feel that our time here has been well spent. The climate is ideal and during our stay the weather has been delightful. The mornings have frequently been misty and we have had several light showers, but there has been but one "rainy day" during the past six weeks. Among the excursions taken while here were two trips to Halemaumau, one around the rim of Kilauea, one to the "seven craters," two to the Twins, one to the Koa Forest, several to Kilauea Iki, several to the Fern Forest, and many about the crater and over the country. We have found several valuable pieces of lava bearing the imprint of ferns, and also quantities of Madame Pele's hair. The exercise and climate have produced enormous appetites, but the table has always been equal to them. Our extended stay here has been made most pleasant by our genial host and hostess, Mr. and Mrs. Bidgood, and their kindness to us will ever live in our memory of this happy period of our lives.

Mr. and Mrs. A. M. Merrill, Honolulu, T.H.,
16 Aug 1904

Aloha Nui to "Madam Pele" and the finest climate in the Islands.

Mr. and Mrs. St. Clair Bidgood, 25 Dec 1904

The house seems to have been cared for well, the cooking of excellent quality and the service very good. We agree in wishing the new management under Mr. Lycurgus a full measure of success in this his latest undertaking in serving the public.

Mrs. A. H. Harding, Portland, Ore., 12 Jan 1905

In 1904, St. Clair Bidgood departed and was replaced by George Lycurgus and his nephew Demosthenes Lycurgus. Demosthenes ran the Volcano House between 1905 and 1919, and visitors were well pleased with the new management.

It surprises me that so many people who feel in need of a change should go to the Coast, when right at hand is such a delightful resort where for a very reasonable figure one may enjoy a climate unequaled in any part of the globe. The new management are evidently in earnest in their desire to make every guest comfortable. All success to them!

Alex Lindsay Jr., 15 Feb 1905

This hotel—situated as it is amid surroundings that appeal to lovers of nature in her mild as well as her sterner aspects—deserves a continued prosperity, while for students specially interested in the varied phenomena of vulcanism, the neighborhood presents a field of unequalled variety. My acknowledgments are due to Mr. Demosthenes Lycurgus for many kind attentions during my stay.

Henry G. Bryant, Philadelphia, 13 April 1905

Visitors frequently noted the beauties of the forests and trails around the volcano area, and continued to suggest that it be preserved as a national park.

The great scenic types of geographic form should belong to the people, and should be free of access to all; their preservation to posterity may be secured by permanent government control. Kilauea is an instance, and like Yellowstone and Yosemite areas, this region should be public domain. An accommodation house equipped with the requirements which excursions in such a region demand, conducted by one competent to direct visitors to intelligent sightseeing, and on reasonable rates so that those of moderate means may visit and revisit this locality replete with volcanic phenomena, is the need at Kilauea.

G. C. Curtis, 15–23 June 1905

For the admirer of the marvelous; for the lover of Nature in one of her most picturesque garbs; for the seeker after health; for the bon-vivant; for the botanist, the geologist, and the seismologist; here is to be found something or other to interest, to enjoy, and to satisfy. Singular must be the human being who can not be happy amidst such charming surroundings.

Edward Armitage, Palikani, 2 Dec 1905

Not to be outdone by the wonders of the forest, Demosthenes and his staff spared no expense to make every moment spent at the Volcano House an unforgettable delight.

Sunday evening, August 26, a jolly crowd gathered around the festive board at the Volcano House, the occasion being a farewell dinner to departing visitors, the guest of honor being Mrs. Mabel Wing Castle who with her daughter has been boarding at the Volcano House for the past fifty-six days. A long table was artistically decorated with trailing rose-vines, ferns and hydrangeas. The menu was as follows:

SOUP
Cream of Celery
FISH
Fried Mullet   Tartar Sauce
Saratoga chips
RELISHES
Green Olives, Caviar on toast
SALAD
Celery   Alligator Pears
ROAST
Roasted Pig a la Hawaiian
Petit Pois   Asparagus
Mashed Potatoes
DESSERT
Omelette Souffle   Chocolate Cake
Fudge   Black Coffee

Toasts in plain ginger ale were drunk to the guest of honor and the host, both responding appropriately. Others contributed to the entertainment with stories, conundrums, and songs, Dr. Kobayashi of Honolulu favoring the company with a Japanese love song. Each one present helped to make the affair one of the most pleasant events of the summer season.

George Beckly, *no date*

Mabel Wing Castle

Miss Elinor Castle.

Mr. Demosthenes Lycurgus has been our host the past two weeks and deserves all that can be said concerning his care of guests. It is worth while to call attention to a somewhat unusual trait—the ability to handle a large crowd with limited accommodations and but little previous notice. On the fourth and fifth the hotel was almost full of permanent guests. Then came an excursion from Honolulu with about 160 excursionists. All were cared for and so pleasantly managed that no grumbling was heard except in the depths of the crater.

C. H. Olson and party, 19 July 1908

Since my last visit in 1906, many excellent improvements have been made in and about the Volcano House under the management of our host Demosthenes Lycurgus. Modern plumbing has been installed. A new 80,000 gallon water tank at a higher elevation than the old ones and filled by a pump operated by a windmill is a noticeable feature. The Sulphur Steam Baths are better than ever, the vitreous pipe connections having been replaced by wooden tubing, so that one may take a "Steam" at almost any temperature. The buildings appear in a dressing of fresh paint and everything is kept neat and clean under Mrs. McLean the housekeeper. The Trail down to the lava floor has been made easier.

One should visit the Vegetable Gardens. The first is near the V. House, just behind the barn. Here you may collect your lettuce, celery, or cabbage; gather mint and see the passion flower and its fruit etc. The 2nd garden is on the trail to the Fern Forest. Take the first road to the right on the trail, a little beyond the R. R. crossing, and wander along with Tree Ferns, Ohia Trees, Ohelo Berries, etc. on either side. This garden is a clearing in the dense forest, covers over an acre and has sweet corn, celery, rhubarb etc. and is half an hour's walk to it.

W. L. Howard, 20 Aug 1908

William T. Brigham contrasted the improved Volcano House and trails in 1908 with the situation in 1864.

At the request of our most kind host I break my custom on this my fortieth visit to Halemaumau, to note not merely the activity of the volcano, which reminds me of the condition in 1864, but to the visitor the important change in the creature comforts he now experiences. At the earlier date the main crater was four hundred feet deeper and there was no trail suitable for horse, hardly one practicable for man. For shelter there was a grass house of one room with floor of coarse hala mat, no bed, a cookstove and attendant Chinese but the visitor must bring his own provisions, and water was condensed from the steam-cracks which were then much the same in volume as at present. Later came the frame house of which the present billiard room is a relic much improved. It seemed a great advance and my conservatism was a little disturbed when the present hotel was added. But as we grow in years appreciation of the mere physical comfort also grows, and now after many kind and pleasantly remembered hosts it is pleasant to have such a shelter and to be cared for by Demosthenes Lycurgus and his obliging staff.

I miss the strawberries once abundant around this region but now extinct. The fine looking raspberries do not fill their place; the ohelos are not so abundant as formerly, and some native flowers are nearly extinct. When I came in 1864 to survey the crater and for the first time carried a chain around it assisted only by Hawaiians, provisions were scarce and other visitors rare. Now that after forty years I am again here to collect more of the local native plants, I find abundance, many fine vegetables grown in the hotel kitchen garden. Good enough roads, telephonic connection with the rest of the island, wireless with the rest of the group, gas in the house and hospitality such as is seldom found in hostelries, and guests in ever-increasing numbers.

Wm. T. Brigham, 26 Aug–6 Sept 1908

Several views of an active volcano, the trail by daylight and moonlight and in darkness, a good hotel, a genial landlord, and plenty of rain, what more can we desire?

> Mr. & Mrs. Wm. A. Holman, Philadelphia,
> 12 March 1909

First-time visitors were equally enchanted.

It has all been like some wondrous dream. Never have we found a host more kind and thoughtful for our comfort and pleasure. The guests we found charming, the weather delightful, the scenery beautiful and the volcano magnificent in its grandeur.

> H. B. Meyer, Purser S.S. "Enterprise," 20 June 1909

This to commemorate the visit of the undersigned crowd of good fellows to the hotel, frankly, on this occasion our visit was prompted by the horrible prospect of having to spend a Christmas in Hilo, Heaven forbid that we should endure such agonies, so now we have tramped around the big crater on a bright and beautiful Christmas morn, snapshotted to our limits, descended to the floor of the inner pit there to take more photos, and eaten a Christmas dinner; the day after, the rain has poured down incessantly, forbidding all outdoor trips, so we gathered around the piano and sang some of the songs in the excellent collection of ragged hymnbooks that repose upon the top of it.

> J. Bennet and party, Dec 1909

It is a question in my mind which was more active, "Kilauea" or the flies. However, I understand the weight of opinion among the guests is that the flies were more active, "Kilauea" not being ubiquitous.

> J. B. Gilman, Lieutenant, U.S. Navy, 6 Oct 1910

Some visitors made witty remarks, including comments on the strange phenomenon of occasional hordes of flies.

Right you are Lieutenant! The crater looked like Hell whereas the flies were hell.

> *signature illegible*, 6 Oct 1910

> One waiter for forty-four of us
> Thank God there were no more of us.
> > *no signature*, 6 Oct 1910

The wonders of Halemaumau is only exceeded by the length of the miles leading thereto from the Volcano House.

Dr. W. W. Irwin, Moose Jaw, Sask., 28 Dec 1911

The two wonders of the world are first the volcano and a waiter who can serve twenty-five guests at the same time and get away with it. Both are wonderful.

Ed B. Webster, Oakland, Cal., 24 Oct 1913

After gazing into the fiery depths of Kilauea, one must consent that the Volcano House Company stands unique among financial undertakings. They have capitalized Hell, and seem to be getting away with it.

John M. Pierce, Honolulu, 24 April 1917

Perhaps the most frequently repeated comments throughout the Register have to do with rain. The following entries, selected from several volumes, illustrate the importance of a good dry hotel.

It appears to be in the habit of raining here.

no signature, 20 Dec 1865

Arrived yesterday from Keauhou. After passing the Panau cross-roads the weather became thick and rainy, and continued so the rest of the afternoon and all the night. Only got occasional glimpses of the crater.

Abr. Fornander, 30 March 1869

Formerly of Pittsburgh, Pennsylvania. Now in Another Hell. It is still raining and has been raining for four years.

C. D. Collins, 18 May 1911

Underneath, the writer came back and added the weather reports for subsequent years.

Still Raining! May 19th 1911
Still raining, July 31, 1916
Still raining harder than ever, February 17, 1918
Still raining April 7, 1920

[40]

Considering the "Mauna Kea" and the roads to say nothing of the cloud-burst, thunderstorm, and lack of sunshine, we all decided that the trip was at least worth making but when we come again, "the weather man" must do better. 8:30 A.M. – 10 P.M. It has rained. Still raining. Wind blowing. Cyclone. Tornado. RAIN. Do not forget your raincoat, umbrella, rubbers, and complete change of clothes as most embarrassing to parade the halls in borrowed kimonos. Bargain Day! Cyclone, Cloud burst and Volcano all for one price!

H. M. Weir, Melbourne, Australia, 14 Feb 1918

To have seen a moon rainbow for the first time in my life, and also to have been treated to the experience of having one side of my head being burned by the sun and the other side of being rained upon simultaneously are the outstanding features of my visit here.

J. Klaykemp, 18 July 1921

I went on a hike to the tree fern forest and got lost. It was pouring rain and it was a miserable time.

Miss Edwina Embree, *no date*

Some visitors were lucky enough to be present when scientists such as Professor F. A. Perret were visiting, or were able to spend time with Dr. T. A. Jaggar of the newly established Hawaiian Volcano Observatory.

Eleven days of pleasure and some unexpected delights—five trips to the crater—an illustrated lecture by Prof. Perret are among the treasures of memory to be relived again and again.

Anna P. Dodge, 4 Oct 1911

We have taken all of the many interesting tramps about the Volcano House. On Aug 2nd a large party, headed by L. A. Thurston explored the lava tube in the Twin Craters recently discovered by Lorrin Thurston Jr. Two ladders lashed together gave comparatively easy access to the tube and the whole party, including several ladies climbed up. No other human beings had been in the tube, as was evidenced by the perfect condition of the numerous stalactites and stalagmites. Dr. Jaggar estimated the length of the tube at slightly over 1900 feet. It runs northeasterly from the crater and at the end pinches down until the floor and roof come together. The tramp is an easy and very interesting one, which every visitor should take.

Wade Warren Thayer, 7 Aug 1913

Visitors continued to note the need to make Kilauea a national park. By 1916, the government had heeded the interest.

As one of the Congressional party to Hawaii—I desire to express my appreciation of the splendid courtesy and and hospitality to the party by the people of the Islands. I am much impressed with the beautiful climate, the glorious bloom and foliage on every side. The enterprise of the people, as evidenced by road construction, is to me a wonder. On my return to Washington, I shall urge such action on the part of Congress, as may establish this in a National Park.

James E. Martine, U.S. Senator of New Jersey, 9 May 1915

The wonder of the world and deserves to be made one of our great National Parks.

Wm. G. Brown, Kingwood, W. Va., *no date*

An indescribable wonder! Such a natural glory should be a Government Park and conducted for visitors as such. The better it is known the fonder the people will be of its possession.

signature illegible, no date

It is hard to keep silent before such marvelous views, and yet silence is about the best description of such awe inspiring wonder. I hope the National Government will acquire and adequately maintain Kilauea and the large volcanic tract surrounding her as a great Park for all the people for all time.

Edwin Dinwiddie, Washington, D.C., 16 Nov 1917

We enjoyed the trip to the volcano. The new section of the Hotel is quite an improvement over the old Hotel.

D. F. Turin, 6 Nov 1921

We are requested to insert our "impressions" in this book. Impressions are good, but the best is the one I make on the mattress when I get into bed on a cold night, when the mist is rolling down from the mountains and the wind is howling around the Hotel like a lost soul.

T. A. Simpson, Waianae, *no date*

Most of us take for granted the scenic beauty, climate and awe inspiring settings of Hawaii National Park. The outstanding feature here is the genuine, homelike hospitality of the Lovejoys—a cheery welcome that sets one at ease, a farewell that causes regret to go.

J. A. Morrow, 2 Jan 1927

Returning after visits in 1923 and 1924. We find the Hotel much improved. The beds delightfully comfortable. The table and service excellent. It is a pleasure to meet again our genial Host Mr. Lovejoy, who gave us cordial greeting and shows interested solicitude for our comfort.

Joseph B. Jamieson, Newton, Mass., 18 May 1927

I shall remember my days here with great pleasure. The first time in travelling (India, China, Japan) I have been able to sit in the woods, enjoy peacefully the birds, the ferns. It reminds me of my own Dorset homeland. Beautiful Hawaii.

Wm. George, Dorset, England, 28 Aug 1927

In 1919, Peter Anastasopoulous took over as manager while Demosthenes Lycurgus went to Greece for a visit. Demosthenes became ill and died in 1921. The Inter-Island Steamship Company then gained control of the Volcano House by purchasing $62,000 worth of stock in the hotel from George Lycurgus. This company made extensive alterations, including moving the 1877 building (the present Art Center) far to the back. Fortunately, this "relic of kamaaina days" was not destroyed when improvements were made to the hotel. Peter T. Phillips was manager for awhile, and was replaced by Channing J. Lovejoy in 1923, who managed until 1927.

Here first in 1899—but miss today the quaint old "Volcano House," with hewn rafters, now relegated to the back yard. Don't destroy this relic of Kamaaina days fifty–sixty years ago.

A. P. Taylor, Honolulu, 19 Aug 1928

From 1927 to 1932, James N. Gandy and his wife ran the Volcano House.

Our best Aloha to Mr. & Mrs. Gandy and their "Volcano House Family"—A 100 percent perfect organization.

H. E. Davies, 8 Dec 1928

The most enjoyable Christmas I have spent in all my eighteen years.

Dewey G. Barnes, Elliott, Iowa, *no date*

I highly recommend the Volcano House and district as the best health resort in the world. I came here on December 14th 1928 run down in health, and very depressed, after two years of sickness, weighed 144 pounds, leaving here after two months in the best of health weighing 164 pounds, the climate is of the best. The food the best I have ever had in any hotel, the service very good, and the comforts of the guests are very well looked after by the Gandys, they certainly are wonderful people. May God bless them always.

James F. Clark, 9 Feb 1929

Such unique scenery, a race which has lived by itself, yet demonstrated sterling character without their neighbour's help and then the warm welcome extended to visitors in these days give a charm to these islands which cannot be duplicated elsewhere. Kilauea is a paradise in itself.

Henry G. Ives, Amherst, Massachusetts, *no date*

Why try to describe Nature—or Pele—who are beyond all words? And who need no praise from us. Let's say a good word for the Gandys—who serve two, or two hundred, with equal readiness and satisfaction.

C. E. Matterson, 13 March 1929

The most spectacular sight I ever hope to see—came to stay a weekend, decided to stay two weeks.

Clare Bennett, 27 July 1929

We've come again, and are about to leave. Friends in Hilo say, "Why go to the Volcano Hotel," to which I reply, No better hospitality is offered,

No better comforts, No better scenery and atmosphere. A home within a hotel.

> Lady Florence, 10 May 1931

We have experienced the greatest of thrills—making a "hole in one."

> Ellen Bacon, San Francisco, *no date*

Here is a word of thanks to the ranger who took us across the Crater. We enjoyed his interesting talk and admired his patience. We hope to meet many more of his type on our travels around the Islands.

> J. Dewenter, Hollywood, Calif., 12 July 1931

Hawaii shines resplendently among the gems which are our National Parks.

> Dr. George C. Ruhle, Park Naturalist,
> Glacier National Park, *no date*

Hawaii National Park is a wonder that is worthy the attention of any world traveler.

> *signature illegible, no date*

The Volcano House and surroundings are tremendously attractive. A visit to Hawaii National Park should not be missed by anyone who has an opportunity to make it. The original Volcano House is especially interesting.

> Major H. J. Ballantine and wife, 30 June 1933

A place where one can revel, wonder, and live in happiness and peace with charming friends and company, is "The Volcano House." A house which is ideally situated high above the majestic crater, now quiet and resting, only to someday come to life again in all of its glory. Every minute of the day can be spent in learning and seeing new things. Such wonderful sights were seen that I really gasped at them. They will truly live in my memory forever and I will never forget the Volcano House and my wonderful friends Mr. and Mrs. Lycurgus.

> Mrs. Constantine Marinos, 19 July 1933

Many thanks to Mr. Nick Lycurgus [*Nicholas, George's son, was assistant manager*] for his wonderful willingness to show us around the National

Besides praising the Gandys and the improved Volcano House, visitors were most impressed with the national park and the rangers, even enjoying the temporary putting green on the brink of Halemaumau—a short-lived arrangement, because the rangers soon began to notice golf balls on the crater floor.

Unfortunately for the Inter-Island Steamship Company, Halemaumau ceased activity in 1924, only two years after they had purchased the hotel and spent $150,000 in renovations. Naturally, there were considerably fewer visitors to the hotel without the draw of a boiling lava lake, and revenues fell. The depression following the 1929 stock market crash deepened Inter-Island's financial problems, and the Volcano House went into receivership. At a sheriff's sale in 1932, George Lycurgus became owner of the Volcano House once more; as the only bidder, he bought the hotel for $300.

Park and the different Volcanoes. I enjoyed every moment of this exciting trip. Thanks to Mr. Lycurgus and his family for being so anxious to see us and for their wonderful hospitality. Such friends will never be forgotten, will always be remembered every moment of our lives. Kilauea is a real beautiful place to live. I could live here all my life, and admire the beautifulness of this unforgettable place.

Mr. Constantine Marinos, 19 July 1933

In 1933, George Lycurgus made a speech that was broadcast over KGU radio in Honolulu. The text was pasted into the Register and is partially presented here.

I am very glad to have this opportunity to say Aloha to my many kamaaina friends in the Islands. Many of our friendships date back to 1904 when I first took over the management of the Volcano House. In those days you came over from Honolulu on the Wilder Steamship Company's steamer Kinau. You came up from Hilo by train as far as Glenwood and then on to the Volcano by horse and stage. Demosthenes with his ready smile greeted you at the door. Old Alec ready to guide you and Peter always on hand to attend to your comforts in the way of coffee and sandwiches; every preparation ready for your first view of the Volcano at night.

I can recall many exciting experiences and good times you and I have had at the Volcano House. Those were the days when the billiard room was a bed room. One amusing incident as to the billiard table was in 1910 when there was great activity here. An elderly gentleman from New York arrived to see the Volcano. The hotel was packed. No place to sleep, poor service and he felt his trip was a failure. He stepped to the office and asked for a mule for the two and a half miles trip over the lava to view the fire. Was told the price of mule was three dollars, then he did explode. "I'll walk, give me a lantern" and away he stamped with the crowds laughing at him. The next morning a different gentleman greeted the crowds. "It was the greatest sight I ever saw or expect to see," he said. "I am staying here a week. Never mind the food or bed, I'll take my turn on the billiard table."

The Volcano House under George Lycurgus became world famous, partly because of the beautiful country and partly because of Mr. Lycurgus himself.

Kilauea and Lycurgus—an irresistible combination.

Homer S. Cummings, 8 Aug 1934

It would be hard to find a more beautiful place.

Dorine Haglund, Honolulu, 17 Aug 1934

What a comfortable place after a hike.

signature illegible, no date

It has been a great treat to return here after many years absence. The officials of Hawaii National Park have so improved the roads and paths that it has been a great joy to drive or walk over them.

Bernice Adele Ross, Honolulu, 11 Aug 1935

I know of no place better anywhere to rest tired nerves and renew one's strength and energy than the Kilauea National Park and the only place to stay if you want good treatment—a real Hawaiian Aloha is with George Lycurgus at the Volcano House.

Lloyd G. Davis, Honolulu, 16 Aug 1935

Such charm, beauty and hospitality I have found at your "Volcano House." I love this place.

Pauline K. Edwards, *no date*

During the last four weeks there have been sunny days, misty days and a few rainy days, but the homelike character of the Volcano House and the geniality of "George" have been the same throughout.

Carl B. Andrews, 6 Sept 1935

Since my first visit to the Volcano House in 1909, there have been many changes and improvements, but "George" Lycurgus remains the same smiling host, always trying to please his guests.

Laura Ann Andrews, *no date*

W. D. Alexander

The Volcano House and Hawaiian National Park is indeed a garden of Eden in Paradise. The exterior and interior of the Volcano House has all the sophistication of the most deluxe Hotel in the world, and yet, by the flickering firelight encircling the cheery hearth, you will find the happy family attitude of a small abode. The engaging smile of welcome and true hospitality, from the most pleasing countenance of Mr. George Lycurgus, greets you each morning, noon and evening. To me this gorgeous spot is like "love"—to describe it makes it but the less. It is something we feel yet can not define. It is something we know, yet can not express.

Fay Frances King, Honolulu, *no date*

We are very much pleased to express our surprise and our pleasure after a short stay at Volcano House. The food was delicious, and the Poha jam—homemade and fresh—wonderful. I wish we could stay, and hope to come back some day.

Lecomte du Nouy, Aug 1937

My first visit to the Volcano House was in 1910 when Old Faithful was performing wonderfully and the heat at the edge of the pit was so intense that we used cardboards with slits to look thru, while our backs froze. My good friend Demosthenes Lycurgus supplied me with a lantern to walk over the lava to the Pit and back at night. George Lycurgus is the same genial host today as twenty-seven years ago. This is the second time I have celebrated my birthday with a cake and candles, thanks to our thotful host. Would that I could remain here more than a month to eat the splendid food and enjoy the cool air!

Laura Ann Andrews, Honolulu, 31 Aug 1937

H. P. Baldwin
Waihee Maui

Many changes since 1918–1923, but more beauty accessible by improved roads and the hospitality even warmer and more sincere.

Mrs. L. H. Daingerfield, Los Angeles, Calif., *no date*

A grand volcano, grand view, grand Guava Jelly and a much grander proprietor—Mr. George Lycurgus!

Eleanor D. Tydings, 20 Oct 1937

To Mr. Nick I have this Toast
To us you've been the Perfect Host.

Mr. and Mrs. J. A. Vanden Heuvel, 1 June 1936

Awe-inspiring scenery—charming host—restful beds—altogether a delightful experience.

Charles Gee, Boston, Mass., *no date*

My first trip to Volcano House. The sight of such a beautiful place will last forever. The best of all was to meet a person like Mr. Lycurgus, his presence makes the place.

Paul Steele, 13 Feb 1947

While I have been on The Islands—and particularly on the big island of Hawaii, I have learned what it must be like to die and go to Heaven. The lovely tree ferns, the marvelous orchids, the softly rolling hills of sugar cane and this Volcano House are parts of a picture that my family will long remember. My Thanks for a grand time.

Clinton P. Anderson, 26 Aug 1947

To Uncle George—A marvelous host, a wonderful entertainer, and a lovable character with a rare understanding of human nature.

Lowell Stackman, Oregon, 17 Sept 1947

You, Uncle George, live joyously in that half-world between heaven and the Inferno—but nearer heaven. We who are fortunate enough to be with you for a rare interlude in what is otherwise a work-a-day world, envy you your rare experience.

Mr. and Mrs. Guy Cordon, 18 Jan 1948

A delightful stay at the Volcano House except for a few interruptions. The last thing at night and the first thing in the morning is a command performance by the genial host to a game of cribbage. I found quite an improvement in George's game since I was last here. His game improves with age.

Peter K. McLean, 26 April 1948

Uncle George: Your fine place is out of this world! I hate to say it, but we haven't got anything like this in Texas.

John Ben Shepperd, Gladewater, Texas, 26 April 1948

A very fine place—just right for a National Park!

signature illegible, no date

In 1940 tragedy struck. A fire in the kitchen ignited the entire hotel. Luckily, no one was hurt, and the park rangers and the C.C.C. firefighters prevented the fire from spreading beyond the hotel to the forest and to other buildings. But everything in the Volcano House was lost.

The 1877 building was spared in the blaze and was quickly spruced up as a temporary hotel. By 1941, Lycurgus had built a brand new hotel, the Volcano House of today. Fortunately, the Volcano House Register was not entirely destroyed in the fire, as most of the volumes were apparently in use in Honolulu at the time, as reference material for a book. The record picks up again in 1946, with more praise for "Uncle George," the Volcano House, the rangers, and Hawaii in general.

To Mr. Lycurgus and the Volcano House, which has the finest view in the world.

Lucille Hull, *no date*

Volcano House. A delightful place to be if you must sit on top of a volcano.

signature illegible, no date

Leaving Honolulu early we saw the beauties of the islands intervening and were certain nothing could be more beautiful. Our guide, Sam, showed us things so breath-taking we were sure there could be nothing left. And then we reached Volcano House—and the view of the crater from there. Indescribable. The host of Volcano House Mr. George Lycurgus was there to greet us and we felt as if we had come home. We think Volcano House should be a "must" on the Matson Tours. There is nothing like it anywhere. We shall leave here with the most pleasant memories of "Uncle George" and his Volcano House.

Grace M. Hurley, Sunol, Calif., 25 March 1949

And don't forget the courtesy of the National Park Rangers.

Ann Hickson, Temple City, Calif., *no date*

It is the most magnificent hotel I have ever seen in U.S. Its views are grand and wonderful I have ever seen in my life. Certainly I shall remember it as the most impressive place I have ever visited.

Kazuo Kawasaki, Osaka, Japan, 21 July 1949

It is always a pleasure to visit with Uncle George the best cribbage player in Hawaii Nei.

Donald B. Harriot, *no date*

George Lycurgus very wittily told me that right here around the Volcano House man can see heaven and hell at the same time. It is truly an awe inspiring sight—the lovely house and its charming host amidst the crater that is still capable to cause death and destruction. An unforgettable experience to me who visited this place before the recent eruption; flew over the volcano during the eruption and now came to see it after the eruption. I hope to be here again and fall in love with the groups of islands anchored in the incomparable blue Pacific and the wonderful people who live here. It is heartbreaking to have to go back to the mainland. George Lycurgus is one of the few men who have made these islands a land of charm and enchantment.

Prof. Boris M. Stanfield, 30 Aug 1950

We are charmed with Volcano House and the fascinating beauty and interest of the National Park. It is a treat to be here and the "sample" is so good we hope to be back soon.

Mrs. Oscar L. Chapman, Washington, D.C., 12 Dec 1951

Oh, to be forever young like my dear Uncle George!

Betty Farrington, *no date*

Note: Information in this chapter is largely based on Gunder Olson's book, The Story of the Volcano House *(1941), and on Frances Jackson's work,* An Administrative History of Hawaii Volcanoes National Park, Haleakala National Park *(1972).*

Three

GETTING THERE

"Road in miserable condition; the worst one I have ever been over."

TOURISTS WISHING TO VISIT *the Volcano House today can reach their destination with speed and in comfort. Air flights from the West Coast take just a few hours, the drive from Hilo takes half an hour, and an extensive system of roads and trails allows easy access to most of the sights in the park.*

It wasn't always this easy. In 1865, mainland visitors wanting to see the lava lake of Halemaumau had to travel for days across the Pacific to Honolulu by ship, then spend a couple more days getting seasick on an inter-island steamer that would land them in Hilo; after that it was a nine-hour horseback ride or an all-day walk up a trail generally described as a mountain stream due to the torrential downpours experienced by almost everyone. Many people, due to fatigue or a desire to enjoy the scenery, took two or more days to accomplish this last leg of the journey. Other approaches, via the Puna coastline or all the way from Kona, took even longer.

ɾ̃

From Hilo, three days ride via Puna, on a very good road. Compliments for J. E. Richardson and Co.

Gerrit P. Judd, 6 Aug 1866

Arrived at the hotel at or near noon only two days from Hilo. Verily I say great is the endurance of that noblest of beasts—the horse. While on the road from Hilo the following will be found excellent: every two hours take out your flask and pour out a little brandy, it then behooves you to contemplate the beauties of nature. Should it rain hard on this most perilous of journeys, I would suggest the propriety of using the above prescription at least once every hour. If the stomach is unable to stand this my advice is stay at home and make those around you happy.

Paul Hunt, 26 June 1866

Many travelers found novel ways of coping with the hardships of the road.

They first observed that the road was rather bad—and in a very short time three of the party observed that it was a "long time between drinks," so the "swill" was produced and after partaking thereof, observed that they felt better. The two latter observations were then repeated during the rest of the journey to the exclusion of everything else. As we proceeded the roads improved wonderfully, so that we found no trouble in coming along at a rapid canter.

B. H., 29 March 1868

Fellow travelers, I left Hilo yesterday with the expectation of viewing the volcano on my way to Kau. Reached here after 9:30 P.M. after twelve hours ride. There was a heavy mist set which rendered it impossible to distinguish an object two fathoms from you and continued so all night. They told me in Hilo that there was a volcano in those parts but as I have not seen any thing that looks like one except some pieces of brimstone which might have been brought from France for all that I know, I have my doubts about there being a volcano here. I will now take my departure for Waiohinu if I can find my way through the fog and remain as wise as when I came.

J. T. Walsh, 11 April 1868

Arrived at the Volcano House in a storm of wind and rain, all of us thoroughly drenched. Found by our journey from Hilo that the people of this island are quite facetious regarding distances, any of their miles being equal to five and a half of those of civilization. The volcano is worth the misery experienced in reaching it by sea and land; and, I think, that is much to say of it.

A.M.M., 2 June 1868

Most travelers in the early days complained about the road, the weather, the boat ride, and the distance, but the sight of the volcano repaid them for the misery of the trip.

[53]

Our "voyage" up, all wet through to the skin

Arrived from Hilo, stopping at the halfway house over one of the worst roads ever seen, with a feeling that some saddles do not fit the human form and that many valuable suggestions might be made to those whose occupation is to manufacture the articles above named to their general improvement.

S. C. Powell, 23 June 1868

I have just returned from the crater. The sight I saw has repaid me for all my trouble, including a twelve days passage on Foster's Fast Sailing Brig Kamehameha IV. Six days confinement at Hilo, on account of heavy rains, and the never-to-be-forgotten twenty-nine miles from Hilo. The accommodations at this house were beyond my expectations.

Henry J. Agnew, 4 March 1871

Arrived about 3 P.M. from Keaiwa after a tedious ride and frequent differences with one of the most mulish mules that ever had long ears.

The heavy rains that had fallen during the three days past had obliterated all signs of the trail and I lost my way in the low ground beyond Uwekahuna.

A. G. Nichols, 4 Nov 1872

Arrived yesterday from Hilo after a ride of eleven and a half hours.

Isabella Bird, 31 Jan 1873

Having found our way here from Hilo without a guide, we presume to relate our experiences. The journey from Hilo is estimated at thirty miles but I consider the amount of hard work that I did in the way of persuading my horse the road ought to have been at least fifty miles. We started at 9:15 Thursday A.M. and succeeded in reaching the halfway house at 2:15 P.M. and were very much disgusted to find that we had only travelled thirteen miles in five hours. Well, we made the best of a hard case and dismounting rested a little while and then attempted to partake of some (what they called) chicken and coffee and crackers, and we retired for the night to our bed, that is, we shared the bed with the fleas. At 3:30 we began to arise and shake off dull sloth, and Mr. Morpheus and the fleas &c &c which took half an hour to accomplish. We were just five hours doing the fifteen miles. When we reached this hospitable roof we were very anxious to interview the cook and ingratiate ourselves into his good books.

Henry Brooke, 9 July 1875

We arrived here yesterday at 2:10 o'clock from Kona, a ride of 100 miles. I had been taught to believe since my earliest recollections that the road to the lake of fire and brimstone was broad and smooth, easy to travel, with plenty of company. We therefore started with bright anticipations of a very pleasant trip, whatever met us on our arrival, but alas, they were not verified in our case, our road was rough, rocky, and narrow, and our party appeared to be the only one on the road at the time. Even the elements assisted in making our trip unpleasant, it rained and the wind blew and on the whole we were very thankful when we arrived here at the house and sat down to a comfortable fire. We visited the sulphur bank and I was so delighted with it that I thought the sight of it alone would well repay me for making the trip. We went down into the crater today, had a good view of two lakes of molten fire, besides several hot places, we got some nice specimens, and returned in the rain, got here very tired,

[55]

wet, cold, and hungry but feeling well repaid for the trip, and prepared to say we had seen the most wonderful fire in the world.

Adela Day, Daisy Day, 12 Jan 1876

Arrived at Volcano House with the first ox cart from Waiohinu to Kau.

L. R. Macomber, 12 March 1877

No fire in Halemaumau my usual luck.

S. W. Wilcox, Kauai, 2nd visit, 5 May 1877

S. W. Wilcox

One of the more humorous habits of Volcano House Register writers was to state the obvious, by beginning entries with "I arrived." Later writers, including Sanford Dole, occasionally made fun of this habit; he found it amusing that visitors would state exactly how many hours and minutes it took them to reach the Volcano House.

Mr. S. W. Wilcox and I arrived yesterday from Reed's Ranch, Kapapala, Kau, Hawaii, Hawaiian Islands, at four minutes and sixteen seconds to two o'clock P.M. The road was stony and uphill—a railroad from Reed's Ranch would be a great accommodation to travellers besides materially adding to the business of the Volcano House. On second thought, we find that we have made a mistake about the time of our arrival—it was three minutes and fifty-nine seconds before two o'clock.

On the day and evening before we came there was a vigorous outbreak on the southeast side of the main crater, a fissure extending from the crater floor through the bank and into the woods beyond. The lava spouted up from this crack to the height of from fifty to one hundred and fifty feet. For adjectives suitable to the sublimity of the scene, see Worcester's Dictionary—anything the intelligent reader may select cannot be too forcible. This action, which drained Halemaumau as dry as an ash heap, ceased just before our arrival. Mr. Wilcox says that it is just his luck. As it is not just my usual luck I am disappointed. We gazed into the empty goblet-shaped cavity called Halemaumau, with a feeling wherein terror was mixed with our disappointment. The ledge on which we stood was separated from the main rock by a deep crack, so that it appeared to be tilted over the hole and already to tumble in. Avalanches of stones were thundering down the sides of the hole which appeared to be about 250½ feet deep. The bottom was covered with boulders. It was some compensation to discover that the pit is not bottomless as has been heretofore supposed.

P.S. We have ascertained that we were wrong after all in stating the time of arrival. The real time was 2.9 and one second P.M.

Sanford B. Dole, 6 May 1877

I arrived here at 3:30 P.M. I am two hours and forty-five minutes behind my time and this is all that I can account for my being so long on the road I met a pest of a man that almost talked me to death and I did not understand as much as where he was going to and I am sure he understood very little of what I said this is my fifth time here.

G. B. Hurst, 20 April 1878

Left Hilo at 8:30 A.M., spent one hour at the Halfway house and arrived at the Volcano House at 8:30 P.M. wet to the skin of course. The road was bad but the horses were—well words cannot express how bad. Were rewarded for our wretched experience by a good flow of lava in the crater and moderate activity on the part of the volcano. Enjoyed the sulphur vapour bath and our stay at the hotel.

R. A. Macfie, Jr., Liverpool, England, 12 Jan 1880

First visit. Left Hilo 12 m. March 29th. Arrived at halfway house 4:45 P.M. Remained over night, and two horses took the opportunity to return to Hilo.

Isaiah Bray, Boston, Mass., 31 March 1880

Left Hilo at 7:30 A.M., arrived at Volcano House at 4:45 P.M. Road in miserable condition; the worst one I have ever been over.

Fr. Specher, Remagen on Rhine, Germany, 12 July 1880

The above represented party left Hilo on foot at 5:30 A.M. July 13, arriving halfway house at 12 m., where we remained for the rest of the day and night. We were most cordially received by the fleas. At 6 A.M. Tuesday we set forth with the remnant of our bodies for Volcano House and reached there foot sore and weary at 1:45 P.M. Spent the rest of the week

As later entries show, however, the habit of keeping track of arrival times did not lessen, despite Dole's parody.

visiting the crater, picking strawberries, raspberries etc. The time passed most pleasantly owing to the kind attentions of our host.

D. Howard Hitchcock, 13–19 July 1880

Left Hilo on the thirteenth, got caught in the rain for the whole of the journey and I am wet thru, the road is in moderate condition but I have traveled better. My new hat is all spoiled, it cost me by the way 25 Cs in Hilo, and I regret the loss as it was important for me.

E. B. Thomas Esq., 15 Aug 1881

Visitors continued to come from Hilo, but by now could also land at Honu-apo Bay, Punaluu, or Keauhou Point in South Kau, coming up to the volcano by way of Pahala and Kapapala Ranch.

Arrived on Saturday night eleven o'clock after a long and tedious ride of about fourteen hours from Hilo.

Saml. C. Damon, 16 Jan 1882

Our party of four left Honolulu Thursday at 4 P.M. and arrived at Honu-apo at 7 A.M. Here we were delayed a few hours waiting for our horses which we thought they had gone to the Volcano House in search of. At ten thirty the much longed for animals came in sight and we could have been seen gazing at them with longing eyes, wondering which would fall to our lot. We were not kept long in suspense for one of our lady compan-ions being a good native talker bore off the prize and the rest of us were favored according to our good looks. This means that the writer had the worst old horse on the island, whose only good trait being that he could always be found at the rear end.

Nevertheless the ride was enjoyed very much, until we had gone some twelve miles when we began to feel the need of rest which we found with a lunch that we all voted the best we had eaten for many a long day at the hospitable house of Mr. Whitney's. Soon after we were on our way to Kapapala where we stopped at the house of Mr. Pracht whose kind and hospitable treatment made us feel at home immediately. The next morn-ing we mounted our horses feeling fresh enough to undertake the sixteen mile journey to the Volcano House where we arrived at twelve o'clock noon.

Today, Thursday, we bid farewell to our kind host, Mr. Lentz, and shall again mount our horses for our down hill journey and from the door can be seen our party, the guide ahead, the writer behind, but who for all that will be gazing with the rest of them for a farewell look at the volcano.

Jeannette Shaw, San Jose, Cal., 10 Dec 1882

Left Pahala yesterday, lost my way. Arriving in the vicinity of crater after dark wandered about for an hour or two in vain effort to fetch Volcano house; finally camped out. Found this very cold. Arrived 6 A.M.

Chas. H. Bragg, 29 June 1883

All very fine, but I do not like the ride up here. My first visit and I think will be the last unless they get a railroad up. Go and see the house of everlasting fire by night.

L. Woodward, Minneapolis, Minn., 4 Feb 1884

Left Hilo at half past ten A.M. and arrived at Volcano House at 2 P.M. This would be remarkably good time but for one trifling circumstance — the leaving time was yesterday and the arriving time today.

John Jay Dickey, 8 March 1884

First passenger through by stage from Pahala to Halfway house.

W. E. Dean, San Francisco, Cala., 9 July 1884

Ye pedestrians leaving ye half way house.

This is the main road Honnapo to Pele's Domain traveled on March 12, 1905

Arrived today from Punaluu at 4:30 having left Honolulu on Monday at 4 P.M. We have found the journey from the start very pleasant and the transportation from Punaluu to this place exceptionally grand. Our only surprise is that a wagon road has not been made from Punaluu to the Volcano House. We have found the quarters here comfortable, and the table better than we were told to hope for. Under all the circumstances of a distant market, and uncertain travel, and the new beginning, we could not have expected better. One must be very hard to please indeed, who can not rough it for a few days on wild turkey served with "sauce d'ohelo."

Mary M. Jewett, 23 March 1885

In 1886 the Wilder Steamship Company took over the Volcano House and built a new road from Keauhou Landing (South Kau) to the hotel. This enabled visitors to disembark at Keauhou and travel only fourteen miles to Volcano instead of the thirty from Hilo.

Tourists wishing to visit the famous volcano of Kilauea can now make the trip from Honolulu with all the ease and comfort possible under the circumstances. Procure a ticket of the Wilder Steamship Co. and you will be landed at Keauhou only fourteen miles from the volcano. This part of the journey is made in the saddle or in a carriage as parties may desire. Nearly all the way a well graded road runs through a tropical forest, the beauties and rarities of which are a source of constant surprise and enjoyment. In fact, the three or four hours occupied in the ride is only too brief for the pleasure offered, and we arrive at the Volcano House, not jaded and worn as is too often the case in seeking the rare and wonderful in nature, but actually refreshed by the ride. With the present arrangements for transporting passengers from the landing to the volcano no one need hesitate about undertaking the journey. Our party of nine not only enjoyed every moment of the time we were on the way but were surprised at the excellent accommodations awaiting us at the Volcano House. Everything was done to make the visit enjoyable and we leave feeling that if anyone grumbles at our reception and entertainment, he should be sent to the regions of Pluto by way of "The Little Beggar."

J. B. McChesney, Oakland, Cal., 17 June 1886

After a pleasant sail in the S.S. Kinau, leaving Honolulu Monday fourteenth inst. at 4 P.M., we landed at Keauhou 6:30 A.M. Wednesday sixteenth—thence to Pogue's six miles we had a pleasant horseback ride over a lava trail making an elevation of some 2500 feet—as we climbed the ascent the view of land and sea was fine. En route were cattle and several bands of goats, wild and domestic ones mixed in these lots as we were informed. At Pogue's, we left our fiery steeds and took the noted one-horse cart seating two. The road led through luxuriant growths of ferns and shrubs and groves of the ohia wood, often so dense as to constitute a jungle. The road was more or less guttered by rainwater, more or less uneven with dishing holes and over a black volcanic sand, and part of way mud, making our locomotion a hard pull for our very good horse. As usual at this season of the year we had a good shower of rain.

Shortly after noon we reached this place, our destination, 4,040 altitude, where we were kindly received and every attention given to our wants to make us comfortable by Mr. Maby the manager, and his amiable and pleasant wife, the host and hostess of the Volcano House. The afternoon was rainy, which kept us mostly indoors, where we enjoyed the comforts of a large blazing and cheerful wood fire.

Fortified by a good lunch, at 2 P.M., we started with our guide David, for the lava basin and crater in the southwest quarter of it. After a walk of some three miles, down the bluff and over the undulating and hilly lava trail, which is twisted and distorted into all conceivable forms and shapes, with innumerable chasms small and great, and caverns gaping wide, we stood upon the brink of the crater, gazing down into the abyss below.

N. H. Davis, Brig. Gen. U.S. Army ret., New York City, 18 Feb 1887

Our party of three arrived here at about 11 A.M. after a remarkably pleasant sea trip on the "Kinau" and a charming ride and drive from the coast. I consider the journey one of pleasure, without a single hardship to endure, especially the time over the last eight miles, the road being quite as good as many around and near the city of Honolulu, if indeed in many places it is not superior.

Geo. Bixby, Long Beach, California, 28 Sept 1887

From the boat landing at Punaluu, visitors traveled to Volcano House via Pahala, often stopping at the Halfway House for rest and refreshment.

I cannot speak too highly of favors received since leaving Honolulu to come to this place. Mrs. Wm. Wilder came on board the Kinau with friendly greetings. The King also came with renewed assurances of good will. We were pleasantly rocked in the cradle of the mighty deep for two days and two nights, meanwhile receiving every kind attention. We thoroughly enjoyed our horseback ride up to the halfway house when we were refreshed by milk, coffee, bread and butter provided by our handsome hostess and then enjoyed our drive in carts accompanied by our gentlemanly and very interesting cavalier host to the Volcano House. Here we find a delightful resort.

Mrs. B. F. Wicke, 5 Jan 1888

Left Honolulu August 28 P.M. on the "W. G. Hall," landed at Punaluu 5:30 A.M. August 30. Started for the V.H. August 31 7 A.M., and after a fine ride on cars, bus, and muleback, last of which was best, arrived okay right side up with care at 2:30 P.M.

F. H. Abeel, New York City, 2 Sept 1888

Arrived this date from Pahala. Came by the new road to Volcano House all the way by carriage and am the first visitor that ever came here by carriage from any landing.

H. S. Tregloan, 28 Oct 1888

As more roads were built, expanded, and improved, visitors were delighted, but also wished for further improvements.

Our party of four ladies and four gentlemen arrived here day before yesterday, "the voyage up" having been made in six and a half hours. We left Hilo at half past eleven, having but just arrived in the new interisland steamer Claudine. Two hours brought us to the end of the fine government road, where we left the stage and mounted one mule and seven horses, reaching the Volcano House and comfort at six o'clock. The company's men said we could not get through until long after nightfall, but the intrepid horsemanship of the ladies outdistanced our best expectations and won universal praise.

Chauncey N. Pond, Oberlin, Ohio, 11 Oct 1890

The trip from Hilo was made partly on wheels and partly on horseback, a triple one, several hours. The experience is a pleasant one, when—as was the case with our party—the weather is fine. The impressions made en route include a desire that the "Volcano Road" which has been the stumbling block of several successive Hawaiian Administrations, cannot be completed too soon for the general good of the country.

V.M., Toronto, Canada, 14–16 Aug 1891

Work was renewed on the remaining portion of the Volcano Road at Keawaanakaaha in Olaa on August 13, 1891. The work is principally to be done by prison labor, with an additional expenditure of about one thousand dollars a month. Nine miles of road must be built before a connection is made with the old trail at the cattle pen—from which point it is six and a half miles to the Volcano House.

Wm. N. Bruner, Honolulu, 14–16 Aug 1891

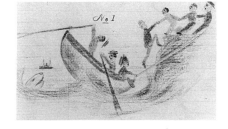

Our route here was by I.I.S.N. Co's steamer "Hall" with good bed and board, a very careful and accommodating Captain, a very smooth and pleasant trip, stopping at eight way ports on Hawaii and three on Maui, and landing at Punaluu thirty-five hours from Honolulu. Found at P a new Hotel, clean and inviting bed and table, a Landlord alive to the interests and comfort of his guests, etc. A ride by Rail of some five or six miles over the most crooked R. Road ever seen brot us to the Pahala Mill where we took stage for the Volcano House.

Of this road from the "Mill" to the Halfway House, eleven miles, I will only say I have traversed worse, and many much better; of the remaining thirteen miles I must say, the man who had the courage, the enterprise, the perseverance and faith to mark out, lay out, and build at his own expense, and for public use, so good a road of so poor material and thro such a terribly rough, rugged, desolate and God-forsaken country, is deserving of a pension in this life and my Daughter says "a free pass from St. Peter."

J. H. Wood, 28 April 1892

The hard, hard trip that one hears so much about, to the famous Kilauea, is at last an experience of the past. Naturally a trip of over 230 miles first by steamer, then carriage, then horseback, then on foot must be at least fatiguing—but as to actual hardships and privations, there are none.

This is surely remarkable when we remember the roads have been so shortly open to travel. Mr. Macfarland of the Wilder Steam Ship Company, Mr. Wilson of Hilo and Mr. Lee of the Volcano House are to be congratulated upon their energy and enterprise.

Virginia Calhoun, Mercury Representative,
San Jose, Calif., 23 July 1892

My first trip here was in December 1888. Every subsequent visit has shown me marked changes in the crater of Kilauea; but what is as well worth recording is the fact that each year has witnessed decided improvements in the Volcano House and the facilities for getting here. This trip has been by far the most satisfactory of any. We drove on the new Volcano Road twenty-one and a half miles from Hilo, leaving only nine and a half miles of horseback riding. And now Mine Host Lee astonishes us with the statement that tomorrow we will ride to the Lake of Fire on horses.

Henry C. Lyon, Boston, Mass., 31 March 1893

Came up today from Hilo. New road excellent, finished to within one quarter mile of Volcano House.

S. E. Bishop, 28 Aug 1894

THE CARRIAGE ROAD
FROM HILO TO VOLCANO
COMPLETED SEPTEMBER 13TH 1894

Dr. R. B. Williams and Mr. F. M. Wakefield, of Hilo, was the first party, who came through to the Volcano by private conveyance, after completion of the Road.

This is my eighth visit to the Volcano House. I had a bad horse so did not get here until 6:55 P.M.

L. D. Spencer, 13 Jan 1892

Some visitors attempted the new roads by bicycle; others made amusing comments about transportation.

At a quarter of nine o'clock A.M. September 13th we started on our Columbia bicycles from Pahala Plantation, Kau, for the volcano. Riding wherever we were able which was about half the time and pushing the rest of the way we arrived at the Halfway House at 12:15. Here we got a good meal and rested. At 2 P.M. started on again and had to push the wheel almost the entire way arriving at the Volcano House at about 7:30 in the evening. In the P.M. of the fourteenth we visited the Lake and again on the fifteenth. Found it quite active but there was so much smoke it was only at intervals the surface of the lake could be seen. We continue our bicycle trip after lunch today for Hilo on the new road which was completed to this point on the thirteenth inst.

W. J. Forbes, David Thrum, 16 Sept 1894

W. J. Forbes
David Thrum.

The noble beast, which bore me to and from the crater, was named Bonaparte, and the other part was the same. He was a small brute, but the law of equalization came in and I, the heaviest one of the party, was given the smallest equine. He had many good qualities, always willing to stop and rest with me, and many a time when I was not so inclined. At such times, he had a bad habit of going to sleep, and with tears in my eyes, I was forced to arouse him. On being violently aroused, the tears were his. He was the most willing horse to stop and rest I have ever seen. He was forgetful, and when cudgeled, would forget that he had been, or for what, before the impression reached his horsey brain and my labor went for naught. As a walker, he was far from fast and my position was soon where I could see the others ahead. I have the impression that he was deaf for he would stop, apparently in fear that I would say "Whoa!" and that he would not hear it.

H. Horton, Jr., Boston, Mass., 1 April 1899

The first trip of an automobile from Hilo to Volcano House. Running time from Hilo three hours, over some of the worst roads possible to find anywhere, the result of the first Hawaiian legislature.

A. James, 12 July 1902

[65]

Some writers described in great detail their journey from Honolulu to the volcano. By this time, a railroad took visitors from Hilo to Glenwood; then a stage took them the rest of the way.

On board the S.S. Kinau, the voyage down the coast of Hawaii was delightful with a smooth sea and fine cloud and sun effects. The approach to Hilo was made by moonlight where we were landed at 8:45 P.M. The absence of rain has been most marked and permitted of a drive from Hilo to Onomea Gulch where the natives climbed the trees for Cocoa Nuts. The next morning we left by trail for nine miles where we took the stage enroute to the Volcano. The country has been changed a great deal in the last few years but enough remains of the tropical forest to make a most interesting trip of it.

The Volcano House is as it has always been a happy resting place where the inner man was generously provided with the best of the market. And now we only await the pyrotechnics of Madam Pele to round out our experiences to the fullest. Tomorrow we go down to Honuapo and board steamer for Honolulu.

signature illegible, 1 March 1901

Left Honolulu on the fine little steamer Kinau January 31. The ride over the rather roughly dancing waves was broken in an interesting manner by stops at various towns and landings, most notably at the ancient capital of Lahaina. At Laupahoehoe we were given a fine exhibition of landing through the surf by the kindness of Manager Wight, who luckily happened to be aboard. From Kohala the scenery equals anything in the world. At Hilo we were met on the dock before the freight was going out of the Kinau, so prompt in action is the management—no loss of time anywhere. All night at the Demosthenes, a good sleep and an early start was made for a ride to Kilauea twenty-two miles by rail and nine miles by stage. The rail ride was through an attractive country forming a panorama of sugar plantations and fields of bananas and coffee. But the particularly enchanting ride was that by stage over a very good basaltic mountain road, walled with tropical vegetation. The useful ohia tree, now and then a rare sandalwood, once in a while a koa, wild bananas, pandanus, graceful tree ferns and a most luxuriant red berry, resembling the raspberry and thimbleberry.

Chase S. Osborn, Sault Ste. Marie, Michigan, 2 Feb 1905

Some impressions gained from a visit to the volcano.

Leaving Honolulu about noon on the Wilder Steamship Company's Special Steamer "Kinau" we spent the afternoon skirting the shores of the various islands of the Hawaiian group and admiring their rugged outlines. Crossing the channel in the night we arrived about daybreak at the shore of Beautiful Hawaii, the giant of the group.

From this time till 1 P.M. we sailed along the windward side of the island. The vista that opened before us on this voyage will never be effaced from our memories. The entire distance to Hilo barring a few miles of rugged mountain scenery was one entire mass of cane fields in all stages of development dotted here and there with settlements around the sugar factories which are a necessary adjunct to the cane plantations. The shore the entire distance is particularly a natural sea wall three to 500 feet high. Over this wall the plantation owners drop their sugar by means of wire cables or other contrivance directly into the vessels that carry their products to the Eastern City. The snow capped summit of lofty Mauna Kea was plainly visible to the naked eye presenting a pleasing contrast to the tropical fields below.

Arriving at Hilo we spent the afternoon very pleasantly in drives around the city. The most interesting being a visit to a plantation nearby where through the courtesy of Mr. Scott the manager we were shown through a modern sugar factory and saw all the processes of manufacture from the cane to the finished product. We were also shown the methods adopted for loading the sugar onto the vessels. We passed for twenty miles through cane fields and banana farms. Our party were all much interested in watching the men and women work in the cane fields. At the end of the rail road we took stages and passed for a distance of nine miles through a jungle of thick tropical vegetation with an abundance of ferns of all sizes. As we neared the end of our drive the vegetation became somewhat less tropical on account of the higher elevation but none the less attractive.

Arriving at the Volcano House a scene was spread before us that can never be forgotten. To the south lay miles upon miles of solid lava where not a sign of vegetation, barring an occasional fern which had obtained a foothold in some of the crevices, was to be seen.

The morning after our arrival we visited the large crater. The distance is about three miles and can be made either on foot or on horseback. In going to the crater we followed a trail down the mountain till we had descended about 1100 feet and then commenced to cross the barren field of lava. Every foot of this trip was very interesting as we beheld the lava cracked and broken into all sorts of fantastic shapes by the cooling process, showing here and there immense fissures and again pyramids or cones in all forms and shapes. We realized for the moment the immense natural forces that accomplished such wonderful results. After crossing over this formation for two miles or more we came to the crater proper. Here we looked down into a steaming cauldron 700 feet deep surrounded by perpendicular walls of solid volcanic rock. This crater has been active at various times lately, notably in 1881 and 1895. We could only wish it was active now but have every reason to be perfectly satisfied with what we saw.

We cannot but urge any person who visits Honolulu to make the trip to the volcano. A visit to Honolulu without a visit to the volcano is like eating strawberries and cream with the strawberries left out. One misses the best part of the feast.

M. A. Moore, 11 Feb 1905

W. H. Shipman

In 1907, the Halemaumau Road was proposed.

The Halemaumau Road—During the visit of the congressional party at this place, Demosthenes Lycurgus, the Host, urged the necessity of a road into the crater. This started the ball a rolling.

Governor Frear soon after his inauguration, gave orders to have the road surveyed. The Territorial Surveyor W. E. Wall sent a man to do this work. And on September 2nd 1907 the work of surveying the road was begun and was kept up through rain, fog and other difficulties until October 2nd on which date the field work was finished and the survey an accomplished fact, making a road of easy grades, about seven and a half miles in length, to be exact, 39,400 lin. ft.

On September 6–7 a party of convicts arrived at the Volcano House from Honolulu, to improve their health and enjoy the climate found here, and incidentally to build the Halemaumau Road. They were employed clearing the right of way and other work until September 23rd and on that date the first actual construction of the new road began and now the work is going merrily on.

A note at the bottom of the page says: Road finished July 26, 1910.

C. H. Smith, 3 Oct 1907

We can hardly say our trip to the Island was uneventful—the Mauna Kea and a goodly gale in the channels took care of that side. Our stop for rest in Hilo was fair to middling despite difficulties of accommodation. Our ride by train to Glenwood was replete with interest in passing scenery, to say nothing of the attractions offered by thimbleberries, realized in a small measure at occasional stops. The stage ride for the balance was thoroughly fine notwithstanding bumpy moments. The real and ultimate purpose, to enjoy which the foregoing events were braved, the trip, walking and riding, across the lava beds of the crater of Kilauea, to the living fires of the pit, the inspection of the forces playing below us as though conscious of their power to belch forth and overwhelm us, scarcely admit of written description. We can only hope that every other whose way is directed to the shores of the Islands may find it possible to experience by actual sight the awful and marvelous spectacle. It is well worthy of every effort to see it. Our treatment at the Volcano House has been of the best we could ask and expect nothing better.

C. H. Olson and party, 19 July 1908

That stage ride from the train terminus was not at all conducive to a Christianlike expression of one's feelings, but had a decided opposite effect. Bumping the bumps and hitting every available hard place (no matter how far out of the way) from start to finish, and fearing that the final destination never would show itself, gave me the impression that the distance from start to finish is one thousand and two miles instead of nine miles, and those last two miles were the longest you ever heard tell of in your life. What little chance I did have for a harp and a crown in the hereafter is surely lost to me now, owing to the method by which I silently expressed my feelings during that stage ride, and now since seeing the fiery pit in action I am exceedingly sorry over having lost that chance, small as it was.

Dedicated to the one who first invented the springless stage as a means of conveyance.

H. C. Bruns, 3 June 1909

C. N. Spencer

Meanwhile, people continued to describe transportation to the volcano.

[69]

Everything is fine. Except the roads, and they would make a better sea bottom than anything else.

Cephus B. McCallum, Dallas Center, Iowa,
24 April 1918

Many visitors began to reminisce about the old days, noting great improvements to traveling conditions over the years, particularly the luxury of automobile travel.

My first visit to the volcano was in May 1872. We came then on horseback all the way from Hilo. What a change! Now to come up by train most of the way then by a stage. Visions of the ride under a tropical rain rise up before me of the years long past. What comforts now, compared with the simple necessities of those days.

Mrs. L. H. Phillips, 27 Jan 1909

Thirteen years ago, the occasion of my last visit, my wife and self landed in Hilo and it was raining. Our first dinner in Hilo never will be forgotten. We collected it from various sources. The Hilo Hotel had shut down. Our first dinner in Hilo consisted of a plate of soup, a bottle of beer, and ice cream. It was all we could get. Now, however, porterhouse steaks, lamb chops, frogs' legs, broiled chicken and the like, as well as many well cooked and well served delicacies are procurable, and the Hilo Hotel is about to be reopened under the same management as that of the Volcano House—recommendation enough!

In 1896 the usual method of reaching the Volcano House was by stage from Hilo. At present the stage runs from Glenwood. Hence the agony has been reduced seventy-two percent. The roads are badly in need of repair. It is reassuring to learn, however, that better and more comfortable means of transportation will be put into operation before long, and that the work of repairing the road between Glenwood and the Volcano House will be pushed ahead as rapidly as funds will permit.

E. A. Mott-Smith, 27 Oct 1909

Unusual Interest in
a Side Issue.
March. 22. 1921.
R.T. Kirby. Bronxville. N.Y.

Plenty of room later
at the Volcano House →

327

The guidebook of thirty years ago notes that "the burning lakes of Kilauea are so easy of access that delicate ladies frequently go to their very brink." If this were possible thirty years ago, how much more so now, with the automobile taking one within a quarter mile of the rim? Now, surely Kilauea's day is here, for who can afford to miss an opportunity to see for himself this matchless display of nature's handiwork? How easy! Nine of us left Honolulu at 5 P.M. Wednesday and after a pleasant half day at Hilo we reached the volcano within twenty-four hours! Is there a sight anywhere comparable to this and to reach it with so little hardship?

L. F. Cockroft, Oakland, Cal., 17 June 1910

On March 29, 1886 I made my first visit to the volcano, on foot, with a guide and J. S. Emerson as mentor and friend.

Today I made a similar visit in an automobile and this as much as anything I know shows the progress of civilization and its concomitant luxury in the Hawaiian Islands in twenty-four years. Who would have thought only 10 years ago that in this year of our Lord, one could get within gunshot of the crater in an automobile and yet dozens are doing it weekly.

J.N.S. Williams, Kahului, Maui, 26 June 1910

We made the trip down in an automobile on the beautiful new road, and the scenery along the way is the most beautiful I have ever seen, calla lilies, immense ferns of various colors along the road side, also wild roses and various other wild flowers growing in almost impossible places. Words fail.

Susan B. Quick, Bath, Me., 8 May 1910

Automobile road finished almost half way across from side wall to the pit of fire, a great aid to easy access to the always wonderful lake of fire.

W. D. Westervelt, 19 Aug 1910

When twenty years ago, through toil and flood
We reached the crater's glare
How little did we dream that large-eyed
Motor cars would rush and stare!

Philip Henry Dodge, 25 March 1911

After a stay of seven months at this restful place, I leave on the Kilauea tomorrow. With new sights and scenes each day, the beautiful tramps thru thickets of tropical ferns and foliage, the unequaled horseback rides, following the old deserted trails of the early days, ending at the brink of extinct craters or to an almost bottomless steam vent, the beautiful automobile rides, also carriage rides has been my good fortune to enjoy.

Miss Hart, Seattle, 17 Feb 1912

Whilst Madam Pele has grown stouter and more cantankerous, Mine Host, George Lycurgus, is still the same courteous gentleman as of old, though he realizes as I do, that the good old days, when a person would spend a week here, and go back and forth to the pit on horseback, have passed on, and now the gas buggy whisks you from Hilo, here and back in a few hours.

Chas. J. Cooper, San Francisco, Calif., 3–4 April 1921

The walk to the volcano can be done by anyone—with Mr. Lycurgus, and is more interesting than going only by auto.

Dr. and Mrs. E. V. Rice, 10 Sept 1910

Of course, a few people recognized that enjoying nature could be best done outside of an auto.

Mr. and Mrs. Donald Kaffenburgh, Boston, Mass., made the first regular commercial flight from Rogers Field Honolulu to Hilo on November 13, 1929. The flight was absolutely perfect and we wish much luck and success to the Inter-Island Airways, Ltd., for their future flights.

no signature, 14 Nov 1929

A volcano in eruption! The most stupendous thing imaginable. I came from Honolulu by plane, going back similarly. The only way to travel.

Mrs. Jeannette Rene, California, *no date*

In 1929, inter-island travel by airplane became possible.

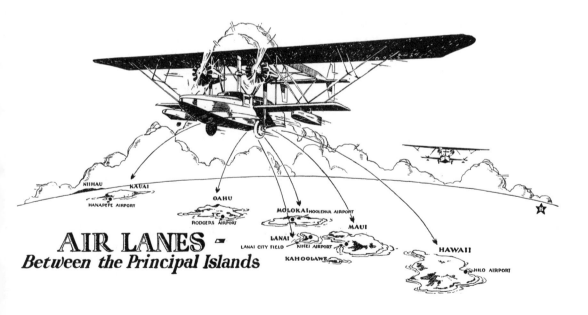

AIR LANES -
Between the Principal Islands

By 1935 the Chain of Craters Road had been built, other roads improved, and trails extended.

We have made quite a number of visits to the volcano and have seen it in most phases of Eruption. My first visit was in 1904 — thirty-one years ago. What great changes have taken place since that long ago date. I well remember coming with two tourists from Chicago, arriving at Honuapo at 7 A.M. one Sunday morning, taking a hack over the plains, no proper road at that time and it took us eleven hours to Volcano House. The same journey can now be done easily in one and a half hours. On arriving at Volcano district the puffing steam gave one a very uneasy feeling. And now the wonderful park, with its marvelous roads and trails; Chain of Craters road now. No road then, only trail, guide, and horseback. They said it was nine miles, to some of us poor riders we always felt it was ninety miles. And the Old Volcano House, we are leaving today, we regret to leave, as we always do, after three weeks of rest and comfort, and we do appreciate the prompt and kindly and efficient service and the spirit of, "If you do not see what you want ask for it," and if 'tis possible, you will get it. With aloha to all and hoping to return at a not too distant date in the not over-long future. Our children, and now our grandchildren too, are coming to this most wonderful place.

M. A. and G. Day, 31 July 1935

In spite of all the hardships of travel, visitors of all periods appreciated whatever trails there were to reach Halemaumau.

I give my praise to the work of the Hui o Kaluaopele for doing the work of lessening the fatigue of descending to see the lava. The road downward to the mouth of the pit has been made good and one can say the great weariness of the descent has ended, with thanks to Pihea, the Superintendent who led well in this great work for the beauty and goodness in caring for strangers. With great thanks to all for taking care of this work of welcoming well the strangers. With delight. [*Translated from Hawaiian.*]

S. Lazaro, Deputy Sheriff of South Kona, Hawaii,
9 April 1893

The thing that impresses me most, after its magnificence, is its accessibility.

F. L. Sellack, Tacoma, Wash., 31 Dec 1911

We descended into the crater and were agreeably surprised to find solid footing. We were, however, unprepared for the cloud of sulphurous vapor which we encountered just before reaching the larger lake. One of our party came near suffocating, and had it not happened that our guide had a bottle of water with him, the result might have been serious. With such experience as my prompter, I would advise all parties visiting the lakes to take an abundant supply of water.

G. H. Sawyer, 14 Jan 1866

In the morning about nine o'clock we went down into the crater and walked across to the fire. On our way back our guide found some fine specimens of lava. One place we found the lava flowing, there we put some coin in taking it up on the end of our walking sticks to cool.

C. A. Akau, M. L. Akau, E. K. Cluney, K. Lahainaluna,
30 July 1874

To a large extent, the people most helpful in making the volcano area so accessible to visitors were the guides. Throughout the years covered by the Register, guides were described as extremely useful and much appreciated. According to the Register, the guides were strong and brave, supplied water to tourists, rescued lost parties, dipped molten lava samples for anyone who wanted, guided people away from dangerous areas, picked the easiest paths to the summit of Mauna Loa, and were very informative.

Volcano House Aug 30th 1874
Kalakaua R.
S. Kipi, Governor of Hawaii
Juis I. Koakanu
E. H. Boyd Honolulu
L. Kaina Puna
Pitkin Wright Iowa U.S.a

We the undersigned party of eleven including the guide made the descent into the grand crater of Kilauea. We went first to the new lake formed some thirteen months ago, remaining there some three hours and taking lunch, a thing the guide said that no other party had done, and at this lake we saw the grandest sights we ever expect to see.

C. E. Conable and party, 19 July 1881

[75]

Arrived from Hilo at 6 P.M. on Friday last November 23 after a toilsome journey of ten hours. Had it wet from half-way house. Visited volcano on Friday. Was at first disappointed, but guide said "wait!" This I did and witnessed in four hours three grand eruptions, feeling amply repaid by the sight of these, for all my fatigue. Found in Mr. Lentz—what one does not often find—the right man in the right place.

Robert Walker, Jr., Woodside, Leicester, England,
26 Nov 1882

Visited the South Lake again and found a fine display. With Mr. Jordan for a guide we found no difficulty in an evening visit. There is no comparison between an evening and a day view.

Geo. H. Barton, North Sudbury, Mass., 9 Aug 1883

Left Volcano House to explore Mauna Loa on October 14th, I cannot say what course is to be recommended to those who have horses, but those who have not a guide will find it better not to attempt to reach the summit on horseback for the whole upper part seems to be a mass of wild tumbled rocks, over which it is very difficult to take horses for one who does not know the best way.

J. Bryce, 18 Oct 1883

Made a second trip to the volcano. A bad night and very wet. The lamps are far from what they should be but the guide is a capital fellow.

C. B. Godman, 16 Aug 1884

Visited the crater on the night of the sixteenth. Rain was falling almost the whole way and the steam to and fro was intense. The road was a most difficult one to find in such weather, and to add to this our lamps completely gave out when we were half way on our way back. I would record here the excellence of the guide who thoroughly understands his business and no one need to fear that even on the darkest of nights, he will not pull through. The crater (New Lake) was very active indeed and a splendid sight was obtained—one that will never be forgotten by me.

William A. Swan, 17 Aug 1884

31 H. H. Reed, 2nd Wife

Visited the volcano in the afternoon and remained till evening. Halemaumau very active, the New Lake quiet. Our guide most excellent and full of information as regards the volcano.

Mr. and Mrs. W. R. Bagley, Wiltshire, England,
5–7 Dec 1884

We the undersigned having met here at the Volcano House. With Tom Pupuu our good natured guide made the trip to the South Lake this afternoon. The goddess has been doing well lately, giving us a grand show of it. The lava is running from Halemaumau nearly all over the crater. The trip was one that we call a good investment although it rained nearly all the time we were gone.

G. P. Castle, Canada, 4 April 1885

Went into the crater and to Halemaumau at 5 P.M.; remained until 8:30 P.M. and reached the hotel at 11 P.M. Fully repaid by the awful grandeur of the scene for all the fatigue endured. Could not have gotten back at all without Haines the Norwegian guide's strong arm and kind help.

Miss C. C. Gnis, Reading, Penn., 1 June 1885

Guides were not only useful, but sometimes very necessary; visitors ignoring their help often encountered unpleasant situations.

I am profoundly impressed by the awful grandeur of Kilauea when after three unsuccessful attempts to reach the edge of the crater the guide refused to accompany our party until a few of us determined to go without him, started; after us he came and rendered valuable service in making the ascent which was done between two large streams of rapidly flowing lava, scarcely 100 ft. apart where we were afforded a view more grand than all.

C.S.M. Launy, Sheldon, Ia., March 1894

Left Ellis station for the summit of Mauna Loa with the guide Henry Gandell. Reached the camping ground at 6 P.M. Pitched our tent on the edge of the crater, immediately opposite the fountain of fire. The sight was very grand. All of our party were more or less affected with "mountain sickness" and one or two were very ill. Water froze during the night, and all were glad to start down the next morning. Left our camp at 7 A.M. Arrived at the camp at the edge of the woods at noon. Rested, and started again. We felt so uncommonly smart that the party started ahead of the guide and prowled around in the woods (it rained hard) until 5 P.M. when our guide found us and took us to Ellis'.

H. MacFarlane, 9 Sept 1872

This day, March 11th, the undersigned visited the burning lake in the crater, in order to obtain a good view we stood on a ledge, about eight feet wide thirty feet long. Whilst standing there, we heard a swashing sound apparently under our feet, we stepped off the ledge and by the time we had got 10 feet from it the whole fell in with a crash. We leave this record as a warning to future travelers to be cautious and not trust too implicitly to their guides — as the lava is constantly breaking in and changing it is scarcely possible for those most familiar with the crater to know with certainty where it is safe.

L. E. Harris, 11 March 1874

Simple justice to the guide compels me to state that the above party went on to the ledge mentioned in direct opposition to the advice of the guide, who had taken them to the safe place always visited by tourists.

Pele, 17 March 1874

Notice. Parties attempting to visit the Lakes without a guide, will be supplied with the necessary articles on short notice, for a decent funeral, and certificate granted for the Life Insurance Co.'s.

M. T. Donnell, Undertaker of Honolulu, *no date*

Started to visit the Lake, but our guide was deterred by the unusual heat all along the path and dissuaded us from venturing. As we stood upon the lava there came an outflow of red hot melted lava directly across the path we had a few minutes before followed and only 100 yards from the point of wall where the path enters.

R. Stuart Chase, Haverhill, Mass., 8 May 1883

Perhaps the most pleasing service a guide could render was to assure visitors that they were witnessing a truly unique sight, for the lava lake just then was "unusually active."

Late in the evening, the clouds were brilliantly illuminated from the volcano, indicating great activity. In the morning we descended to the "Burning Lake" and our guide informed us that it was unusually active.

K. Lorita Valentine, Waikapu, 31 Aug 1865

According to the evidence of the guide the volcano was more active than he has ever seen it before.

F. I. Mathews, Chap., HMS "Opal," 10 Dec 1878

In the evening when we left at eight o'clock, there were two remarkably active but intermittent jets near the west wall of the north lake, throwing out masses of lava from five to twenty-five or thirty feet. The guide said it was by far the finest exhibition he had seen since last March. He was even quite enthusiastic over the display.

J. A. Zahm, C.S.C., Prof. of Physical Science,
Notre Dame Univ., Indiana, *no date*

We continued on our trip and arriving at Dana Lake found it in a state of marked activity, the guide informing us that it was much more active than for some weeks past. The scene was grand in the extreme. The entire southern end of the lake was an unbroken line of surging, boiling lava, presenting a spectacle of indescribable grandeur.

We then proceeded in driving rain to the Little Elephant and after forcing our way through the sulphur fumes, we succeeded in reaching the high bluff on the western edge of the crater, from which point we had a most magnificent view of the lake. The guide informed us, that we were the only persons, to his knowledge, that had ventured to that point.

E. C. Macfarlane, Honolulu, fourth visit, 21 April 1889

To see Kilauea is one thing, to describe what you see is quite another. I had my first view on Thursday evening, and the guide said the lake was more active than he had seen it for four months, so I reckon I was pretty lucky. That marvellous cauldron of seething molten lava is alone worth traveling more than 8000 miles to see. I think Albert, the guide, deserves many thanks for the excellent way in which he looks after the troublesome tourist.

Walter C. Peake, Surrey, England, 19 Nov 1893

The Lava Lake, which broke out in May 1880, is 3000 feet in circumference and the sides are fifty feet to sixty feet deep. It is so active at this date, and so brilliant at night, that Rawbuck the guide expects it will soon become much larger.

T. Unett Brocklehurst, Henbury Park,
Cheshire, England, Sept 1880

Mr. Robeck was a very popular guide in the 1880s, although his name was rarely spelled the same way twice.

Arrived here from Hilo. Ceaseless rain all day made the ride hither unpleasant and fatiguing, but visits to the crater the two following days more than compensated for any transient inconvenience, which only served to enhance our appreciation of Mr. Lentz' kind arrangements for our comfort. We were also indebted to our excellent guide Mr. Robeck for his help in guiding us both days into the crater and assisting a somewhat elderly pedestrian in surmounting the difficulties of the ascent in a most efficient manner.

signature illegible, Norfolk, 20 Feb 1882

We went with the guide to watch the flowing lava, and were much interested in what we saw, though we did not attempt to approach the source of the stream; our guide, Mr. Roby, had told us he expected some unusual phenomenon when we visited the crater on the seventh and he now tells us he does not expect this lava flow to continue very long.

We have much pleasure in testifying to his excellent powers as a guide; and we also found him no less pleasant a companion, than trustworthy as a guide. We think ourselves most fortunate to have found so comfortable and pleasant a spot in a place so far from the haunts of men.

Edwin Rushfield, Rev. A. F. King, England, 5–11 Nov 1884

I soon found myself at home here and in the company with Mr. Rorback the most estimated guide to the terrors of the crater I spent many happy an hour. Weather was bright when we visited the crater and I was highly astonished to see such a wonder of nature before me. I never thought such a great admirable sight could be had on this earth. I leave tomorrow very thankful to Mr. Rorback for his kind treatment and his friendly acting.

C. Wiedemann, San Francisco, 22 Dec 1884

Arrived yesterday at noon. Had a good view of Madam Pele: and had a pleasant evening with the affable guide and manager Mr. Roback.

Marvin E. Pack, U.S. Harris, 1 Jan 1885

Another popular guide was Alex Lancaster, who guided visitors between 1885 and 1929.

Our guide Alex Lancaster is a shining success in his business.

F. F. Crowson, Stoneham, Mass., 11 April 1903

We visited the volcano and were much interested in all we saw and found our guide Alec Lancaster most merry and intelligent.

signature illegible, 11 Oct 1906

We the undersigned do hereby testify to the following that at 2 P.M. November 6th 1907 it was our expressed intention to follow the well-

Our guide loses his way.

August 9th 189-
Clear starlight night.

"I little more down this way."

"Patience." on the lava.

defined path to the crater Kilauea-iki. We thought we would follow the little trail to the left for a different view of the pit. After crossing several gulches our trail became less defined and suddenly we found ourselves again at the crater's edge, but alas! on the opposite side from where we started. The hour being late we thought of returning.

We were lost! The hours passed. Near nine o'clock we heard the calls of a party in search. At last the approach of someone became a certainty and suddenly, by the light of a lantern he carried, there approached a man. Surely there was a halo above his head and a smile such as the angels wear on his face. It was the guide "Alec" and thus were we rescued.

Occasionally, of course, things went wrong. The group shown in the above illustration may have had a new or inexperienced guide, or perhaps it was just "one of those days."

[81]

Well to make this long confession no longer, we arrived at the Hotel at 3 A.M., tired and wet but filled with gratitude towards the jolly crowd that rescued us, and should these lines ever be perused by Messrs. Lycurgus, Wall, Deys, Charlie or Alec let it be forever understood we are theirs to command.

Helen Wood, Emma Wagner, Owen Williams,
Wm. Elliott, 6 Nov 1907

When the automobile was invented and good roads were established, guides began driving visitors to the sights rather than outfitting them with lanterns and walking sticks.

Every minute filled with pleasure, to the accompaniment of the song birds, both in the air and on the ground, not forgetting our song bird chauffeur from Hilo.

Mrs. C. Ransom Samuelson, Long Beach, Calif.,
13 May 1930

To the driver of our car
Who ever will be a bright star
He took us to the edge of the rim
Where the outside world in memory grew dim
He left nothing untold
And as a guide on him we are "sold."

Dr. and Mrs. Samuel Wolfe, Phila., Pa., 3 June 1931

Just a few lines to express our appreciation and gratitude to the driver motoring us around Hawaii whose endeavor to make the trip interesting as well as enjoyable will long be remembered.

Martha Wehapp, 11 July 1931

Four

VOLCANIC ACTIVITY BETWEEN 1865 AND 1955

"Kilauea active again!"

MAUNA LOA AND KILAUEA *volcanoes erupt frequently. Since 1865, when O. H. Gulick donated a blank logbook to the Volcano House and solicited comments for the purpose of creating a written record of volcanic activity, visitors have recorded their observations. Many of them strayed from Gulick's original intention, recording instead poetry, notes on trips to other countries, praise for the hotel, and New Year's resolutions.*

In the first volume of this work O. H. Gulick asks for records of observers that may be useful to future generations. It almost seems a pity that a second book was not at the same time placed on the table called the "Wags Book" where poets, quasi artists and wit mongers might entertain their less serious and less thoughtful friends, as this volume seems to have the maximum of light literature and the minimum of scientific records.

There can be no doubt that all visitors to these regions may not only contemplate the vast wonder of creative work but learn a lesson from the master hand on the spot, if simple records and changes are carefully and correctly recorded both of the action of Kilauea and of Mauna Loa.

A.D.B. Fellow of the Geological Society of London,
7 Aug 1896

. . . For some years past previous to 1863, most of the fires visible were to be seen at, or in the vicinity of, the lake, in the southwest part of the crater, but in May or June 1863, there was an extensive eruption in the northern part of the crater.

Since that time, the second or smaller lake at the northern side of the

Yet buried amongst the "less serious and less thoughtful" writings are a great number of outstanding descriptions of volcanic activity, so that O. H. Gulick's plan succeeded after all. Of course, the chronology of eruptions on Mauna Loa is not complete, since some eruptions occurred which were either unobserved or not recorded in the Register. In reading the chronologically arranged entries in this chapter (all of which refer to the summit area of Kilauea unless otherwise stated), it is important to understand that Halemaumau, the summit crater of Kilauea, and Mokuaweoweo, the summit caldera of Mauna Loa, look very different today than they did in the past, due to the lava flows, earthquakes, and subsidences that have altered the landscape.

In 1865, the Kilauea caldera floor was about 600 feet deep, with a molten lava lake 800–1000 feet in diameter at the site of the present Halemaumau Crater. Over the years, the scene changed dramatically, as the lava lake alternately rose, sank, developed cones, and split into smaller lakes. For similar reasons, a map of Mokuaweoweo today looks very different from one made in 1865. The entries in this chapter provide a geologic history of Kilauea and Mauna Loa, from 1865 through 1955, as seen through the eyes of Volcano House Register writers, beginning with Gulick.

crater has been formed—and seems to have become a permanent institution. The two lakes are perhaps a mile and a half apart. There is more or less smoke issuing from many of the cracks in a line between the two lakes.

The island that has been in the large lake for some time past has disappeared.

O. H. Gulick, 2 Feb 1865

For many decades, various "islands" were observed within Halemaumau lava lake, often changing location and appearance. These islands, according to T. A. Jaggar, were part of the "epimagma," the lower, more viscous, aa-like lava deep within the lake that often projected craggy masses up through the more fluid, pahoehoe-like "pyro-magma" above. Some visitors shared Jaggar's view, while others believed that the islands were floating like rafts.

The island spoken of by Mr. Gulick as having disappeared cannot be said to have had any permanent location or size. In the first week of January I noticed the top of the island was nearly on a level with the lake, and upon making a second visit the following week it was located farther to the west bank and was about ten feet above the level of the lake.

J. B. Swain, 8 Feb 1865

Crater filled with several "floating" islands all surrounded by spouting fountains of yellow lava, a grand and magnificent sight. My second visit and have had a glorious time.

F. F. Woodford, Honolulu, 22 Sept 1921

[84]

The large lake was unusually active. The surface of the lake with the exception of these three fountains was covered with a black crust which appeared to have the power to restrain the gaseous heat and force it to find vent through the three fountains. The lake continued in this condition for about one hour when the action became more violent and the crust began to break up. First a crack in the crust was suddenly disclosed several yards back from the cauldron or fountain and in a circular direction around it. The crust thus liberated gushed suddenly forward. It would proceed thus but a few feet when the forward edge would tip downwards at an angle of from thirty to forty-five degrees and quickly disappear beneath the fiery flood while in the place it had lately rested and over the place of its final disappearance there would burst up an immense number of beautiful sparkling jets. A commencement now being made it appeared easy for the balance of the crust to follow suit, and another and another piece would break off, rush forward, and disappear the same as the first, until the entire surface would be broken up and submerged! After this violent action had continued from fifteen to thirty minutes and the old crust had all or nearly all become melted or submerged the lake would gradually become more quiet. The fountains would cease to play except a few around the shore and another crust would at once begin to form which after a brief period of repose would be again broken up in much the same manner as the one I have described.

Chas. W. Marlette, 8 Oct 1865

My previous visit was on the twenty-third of May 1864. At that time there was but one lake of any note. On my last visit (the nineteenth Inst.) the first thing that attracted my special notice was the large north lake entirely new to me as were also several other lakes. Very much new lava has flown over the bottom of the crater and several caves into which I descended in May '64 appear to be filled up as I cannot find them this time.

George Clark, Honolulu, 25 July 1867

My first visit was in 1853, and after fourteen years of continual changing, Kilauea hardly seems the same to me. The bed of the crater is greatly filled up, and the Old South Lake has many new rivals, for we saw the fires of eight last evening.

A. Francis Judd, 18 Sept 1867

An entirely new and quite extensive lake, in an entirely different portion

From 1865 to 1868, Kilauea Caldera contained a large lava lake and several smaller ones. By repeated overflows, these lakes gradually filled the surrounding crater. Mr. Marlette gave an accurate description of a phenomenon called "crustal foundering" which has been seen in more recent lava lakes, such as that which filled Kilauea Iki crater in 1959.

of the crater burst upon our sight. This lake which should be called the new lake we are informed by the present proprietor of the Volcano House first formed early in March 1867 by the falling in of a knob-like cone. Since then it has been steadily increasing in size and brilliancy.

Mrs. S. J. Lyman and Miss M. A. Chamberlain,
20 Sept 1867

On 2 April 1868, there was a great earthquake, which resulted in a mudslide in Wood Valley near Pahala that killed thirty-one people, and Kilauea's lava lakes drained away. Lava poured into Kilauea Iki through a fissure in the crater wall and covered the floor; this flow stopped in a few hours. In addition, there was an eruption on the southwest rift zone of Kilauea, at Nuku Pili, and on the southwest rift zone of Mauna Loa, at Kahuku.

Kilauea is dry, for the first time since 1840, when Kilauea emptied its liquid contents through subterranean conduits in the flow which reached the sea at Nanawali in Puna. This time it seems to have sent them underground a distance of forty miles to rise in the destructive eruptions at Kahuku in Kau. We have today made a full circuit of the crater and not found a trace of liquid lava, not a vestige of the incandescent lakes remaining, in place of them vast pits, with beetling toppling walls, of frightful desolation. At least two-thirds of the area of the crater towards W. and N.W. have caved in and sunk about 300 feet below the level of the remaining portion of the old floor. The bottom of Kilauea Iki, formerly covered with thick vegetation, is now floored with black lava which rose in it between 6 and 10 P.M. on April 4 [*Editor's note: eruption began April 2*].

William Hillebrand, 18 April 1868

Pele has roared again last night. Fire was seen in the south lake at twelve midnight. Reports from Kau have come in that the eruption at Kahuku ceased two days ago.

William Hillebrand, 19 April 1868

*Joseph Moriis
Hilo*

We left Waimea on the eighteenth. Visited the new flow at Kahuku. We found the flow came from an immense split or ravine with quite a number of cones. The lava was hot and steaming on twenty-third. After two days rest there, we made the ranch of Mr. C. Richardson, who received us very kindly, and accompanied us to the new flow at Nuku Pili. We found red hot lava but the flow had ceased. The pahoehoe was quite hot. The flow also appears to come from a split or ravine. The extent appears about a mile I guess or more.

The mud flow near Mr. Richardson's where some thirty-one persons perished is well worth a visit. Mr. Holmes and myself went to the top. I must say it is the hardest walk one can take. The mud flow was caused by the Great Earthquake on April 2nd was so sudden and quick that it could not be seen by those who were within a short distance.

Frank Spencer, 27 April 1868

THE THIRTY-ONE WHO WERE BURIED BY THE LANDSLIDE

> To guard their bones,
> No Shakespeare's curse ever need be said
> No mortal hand will e'er disturb
> Those relicts of the dead
> No pall, no coffin and no shroud
> They rest beneath the sod
> Like Moses on Mount Horeb's height
> They were buried by their God.
>
> *no signature, no date*

When I first saw this crater (September 5, 1866) the action was confined to the North and South Lakes, but it increased gradually, till, just before the Great Earthquake of April 2nd, 1868, there were 12 lakes in active operation, besides many cones. On the night of the 2d of April the appearance of the crater was grand beyond description, nearly the whole surface being covered with the liquid lava. For two weeks after the earthquake there was no fire to be seen in the crater, but it is again in action, and promises to equal its former grandeur — in time. The centre of the crater has dropped all of 300 feet below its former level.

Chas. E. Stackpole, San Francisco, 16 Aug 1868

Memoranda, taken from L. Kaina's lips. April 2nd, 1868. About 4¼ P.M. the great earthquake took place at his residence a mile or more above the Volcano House. At 5 P.M. Mr. Kaina reached this house. The region to the north of the old South Lake had already fallen in, and a great stream of lava was pouring from the South Lake northward into the depression,

Plan of the "Old South Lake"
Dec. 8. 1874

B

Crater Canyon

Present position of
"Lake Kilauea"
now active Dec 8. 1874

Best point of observation

very smoky

A   C

D

Halemaumau
Same position as formerly
In action Dec. 8. 1874.
out active fitter

old point of observation

Position of "Kilauea"
in 1872, as seen by Bridges &
Stevens now
not in action Dec 8 1874
active in 1875

very smoky

Plan of the "Old South Lake" Dec. 8. 1874. — as seen by Wm Whiting.
Estimate measurements —
Lake Halemaumau 300 feet across.
Lake Kilauea — 500 to 600 feet long — 300 ft across
Entire length of the South Lake from A to B. 1500 feet.
Crater Mouth for C to D. 800 feet.
Hight of walls of Lake Kilauea at B. 1000 ft.
  "   "   "   "   "   B. 500 ft.
Distance between the two Lakes — 800 ft.

Dec. 9. 6 o'clock A.M.
Ther. 48°

in a cascade of fire. At 6½ P.M. fire was seen over Kilauea Iki simultaneously with a terrible noise, when the floor fell. There was great noise and
fire in Kilauea till 10 p.m. when the fire went out in Kilauea Iki, and began
to diminish in Kilauea.

O. H. Gulick, 7 Oct 1868

The action of the South Lake has been increasing rapidly during the last
three weeks. On a previous visit Oct 15th, 1868, the South Lake or Pit was
about 250 feet deep. There were several cones in the bottom but not much
liquid lava. On visiting it again today we found the lake had filled up
some 150 feet and the action divided into three different lakes, viz. North,
South, and West.

no signature, 8 Nov 1868

Following the subsidence of 1868, lava returned to the South Lake, and the crater gradually began to fill up, eventually forming a dome-shaped shield at Halemaumau. In addition to the large South Lake, sometimes other smaller lakes would appear, periodically merging with South Lake.

The whole South Lake is now solid with the exceptions of three small
pits where the lava is boiling and there are four small cones. It is also
gradually filling up and will before long become an immense dome as it
was from 1848 to 1868.

D. H. Hitchcock, 10 Jan 1870

Mr. Kaina informs me that on the nineteenth of February the South Lake
overflowed its banks for the first time since the earthquake.

G.T., 6 March 1870

Find a great change in the South Lake. The whole is now filled up and a
huge mound is forming over it.

D. H. Hitchcock, 26–28 April 1870

We were startled by a noise like the report of a cannon; rushing to the
door we beheld a scene of startling grandeur. An immense lake had
formed of what had seemed the first part of the evening, three distinct

[89]

lakes; it boiled and surged in a magnificent style for about five minutes and then cooled down. The Chinaman [*Akona Pake*] says that this same lake was active last week, but that there was a severe earthquake at four o'clock Wednesday morning, at which time the lake sunk, and became three distinct lakes.

A. Frances Johnson, Hanalei, Kauai, 5 Oct 1870

The old "Halemaumau" has assumed the appearance it had from 1845 to 1868, that of an immense dome about 600 feet above the level of the centre of the crater. On its summit are two lakes even full and from which every few hours streams of lava run in every direction.

D. H. Hitchcock, 21 Oct 1872

Mauna Loa erupted in August 1871 for about a month, and again on 10 August 1872, in an eruption that lasted for about sixty days. It is possible that Mauna Loa was in more or less continuous activity from August 1872 until February 1877; the more violent episodes were visible from Hilo.

At half past six this evening, I saw something strange — a cloud appeared on the summit of Mauna Loa — like a trail of smoke it rose straight up. The mountain lay in plain view — the whole brow of it. As I was watching [*the cloud*] issuing forth I was surprised at the extreme redness of it, like a strawberry. It went up almost 200 feet perhaps from the summit of the mountain, then it died down and became like a red mist. Not five minutes later it began to get black, like charcoal.

Seven o'clock. There is very little of this strange thing to be seen on the mountain other than the constant glow. In my opinion it will not be long before the Old Woman will be seen again overrunning the land. [*Translated from Hawaiian.*]

A.K.M., Hilo, 12 Aug 1871

Ascent to the summit of Mauna Loa. We left Reed and Richardson's on the morning of Tuesday September 3. Fine clear night and not cold, and the fires of Kilauea below and those of Mokuaweoweo above us were distinctly visible. Started the next morning at seven o'clock, we arrived at the summit at 1:30 P.M. We found the crater in operation throwing up a fountain of lava from a cone about in the middle, to the height of 150 feet or so, and the lava was running in a stream to the northeast, covering over nearly all that portion of the crater. We decided to remain all night. Weather clear and cold as the sun went down, and we could not keep very comfortable during the night. The thermometer we had was only graded as low as thirty so we could not tell how much below that it went. The view of the fountain and lava flow after dark was perfectly splendid and more than repaid us for the discomforts of the stay — it was continuous all the while we were there, and we judged had not varied any since it first broke out on the 9th August, nearly four weeks previous.

H. N. Palmer, 8 Sept 1872

I visited Mauna Loa. On the twenty-seventh, a jet of lava was playing in the southwest pit generally about 150 feet in height; sometimes it rose to 300 feet or more. The great lake was not agitated but showed a great deal of fire at night. The ascent of Mauna Loa is exceedingly difficult, and visitors attempting it should have good mules and an abundant supply of very warm clothing.

Rev. A. F. White and Mrs. C. T. White, 29 May 1873

I have just returned from a very interesting trip to the crater of Moku-aweoweo on Mauna Loa. After climbing over the most awful road I ever saw, we reached the crater. We went to the northeast point, and looking down the precipice, say about eight hundred feet, over the shelving mass of loose rocks and debris, I thought we might possibly venture to go down. After half an hour's awful labor we reached the bottom which is now entirely covered with the flow of last year. From where we stood the awful walls of rock arose on every side, and it looked as though no human being could ever ascend from that vast depth. We had not time to go to the active south lake where the molten lava was heaving and surging with loud reports and hissing where we entered. There are many blowholes in this field, and from some of them I collected specimens of lava too hot to be held in the naked hand. At night fires can be seen in these holes, and at all times the hot steam and gases rising with a hissing sound. The heat of the black pahoehoe was so great as to blister my feet through a thick pair of boots.

About a mile from where our horses were we came across stone walls that must have been built for the sides of a house or camp. I found an iron eye-bolt and a piece of soft pine, both of which must have been there thirty years. I think this was Wilke's camp of 1841.

W. W. Hall, 22 Sept 1873

The plan of the crater of Mokuaweoweo is from actual survey by triangulation. Its greatest length including the basin at the north end is 17,000 feet, or about 3.2 miles; excluding this it is 15,000 feet; its greatest breadth is 8600 feet or about 1.7 miles; its greatest depth 1050 feet. The floor, however, is continually rising owing to repeated overflows, and the lake is about 500 feet in diameter, and at the time of our visit was quite active.

John M. Lydgate, 24 June 1874

Latest from Mokuaweoweo.

The burning lake itself was less active than reported by the last party, still the action was very satisfactory at both ends of the lake, that nearest the camp the most active, throwing up jets varying in size and height, occasionally throwing up some hundred feet or more.

Any one travelling to see the sights will never know how much may be lost by not going up this hill, until they accomplish it for themselves.

Anyone who takes a delight in becoming familiar with the wonderful workings of the Divine Architect as exhibited in different phases, from the rude beginnings of foundation to the finished landscape will never regret the trip—we firmly believe.

B. F. Dillingham, R. Whitman, 3 Sept 1874

A faint light was seen from here at 9:15 on Mauna Loa.

J. W. Gilman, 21 Aug 1875

Meanwhile, eruptions at Kilauea summit continued as usual, except for a minor subsidence in April 1879, at which time the lava disappeared for a month.

At my previous visits the southwest or principal lake of liquid lava was only from ten to fifteen feet below the surface of the surrounding plain of hard lava forming the bottom of the crater, whilst now I find a cone about one hundred and eighty feet high with the lake of lava in centre of cone and depressed about two hundred feet below the top of said cone. The sight is not so grand now as at my former visits, because then the entire bottom of the crater was much deeper than now, and the lake more brilliant in its action, and being nearer the surface was in full view from the point where the hotel now stands, so that our party were all able to read a newspaper by the light from the lake.

William P. Toler, 1 Jan 1877

The course across the lava beds was very direct, and in due time the South Lake was reached. They found it quite active, and it was of course pronounced at once as a sublime spectacle. The lava was constantly being

Latest from Mokuaweoweo

Sept 3rd 1874

Two wayfaring men just returned from a visit to
the summit of Mauna Loa - for the benefit of science,
or those who come after - have to report the crater
of Mokuaweoweo in the same condition topographically
as reported by the last party and illustrated by
J. Lydgate (P 47) with this correction that the bank
represented in the plot as making nearly direct
from the active lake to the middle camp, really
extends along and joins the bank near or just below
"Wilkes camp."

       The burning lake itself was less active
than reported by the last party, still the action was
very satisfactory at both ends of the lake, that nearest
the camp the most active, throwing up jets varying
in size & hight, occasionally throwing up some hundred
feet or more, the color of the lava appeared to us
very peculiar being a bright vermillion & sometimes
blood red.

       For the encouragement of any who may
desire to see this big thing in the way of lava, we
would state that for any one at all used to riding
the trip is not so much of an undertaking as many
represent. The trip may be made easily in two days
if desired, the first day riding some five hours
and stopping at a goat camp where there is a poor
grass hut for shelter if it rains, if a tent is carried
you will go a little further up before camping, the
next day with an early start - 5½ o'clock, you reach
the crater from 10 to 11 o'clock, leaving about noon
we reach Reeds upper ranch by 5 or 6 o'clock, after
riding over such a mountain of unadulterated lava
as one will probably never find elsewhere, the
character of the lava is "pahoehoe" - smooth rock -
still its arrangement is any thing but smooth
as a white man understands it, you may get
a faint idea of how it looks, if you have ever been
to sea in a storm, or when it is so agitated as to be
called a "chop sea" - imagine a boundless expanse
of this petrified and you get the best idea you
can without seeing for yourselves, this wonderful
sight.

       Parties that stay on the top over night are
almost always affected by the air, and are more
or less sick, but our experience proves that one
may go in the day time and not feel any

thrown up in jets to a great height, some pieces being thrown even as high as the ledges on which our travellers stood.

Godwin McNeill and party, Sacramento, Cal., 8 June 1878

The crater is now very active. There are now as formerly two lakes connected by an isthmus, the old south lake being much larger, and the lava in both rising nearly to the rim around them. But it has not run over the rim, the lava bursting out on one side or the other every few days, making streams which are gradually filling up the central basin.

H. M. Whitney, 7 Jan 1879

Bottom dropped out of Crater.

L. [*W. H. Lentz*], 21 April 1879

Arrived at the Volcano House April 21st '79. Went down into the crater next morning and found the d— thing extinct; having caved in the night before my arrival. Just my luck.

G. Grosener, San Francisco, 22 April 1879

Both lakes very active, Halemaumau throwing jets of lava up at least fifty feet above the rim of lake so often that the lake looks like a fountain of fire from the verandah.

W. H. Lentz, 24 June 1879

In 1880, Mauna Loa erupted twice, and both eruptions were recorded by the Volcano House manager; one eruption continued into 1881.

Nine thirty P.M. Mokuaweoweo—the large crater on top of Mauna Loa burst out in a large lurid light with a roar resembling thunder. 10:05 P.M. a second eruption this time from the crater to the north of Mokuaweoweo—apparently as large as the first. 11 P.M. still another this time southwest from the first making in all three active fires on top and slope of Mauna Loa. Kilauea very active, both lakes booming, a third forming—several large flows on floor of crater.

Wm. H. Lentz, 1 May 1880

Gerrit P. Wilder

About 9 P.M. November 5th a flow of lava started from the northern slope of Mauna Loa—apparently toward Waimea—or Hilo, and is still running.

On November 9th about 8 P.M. the above flow started a branch along the slope and face of the mountain towards Kapapala Ranch, Kau, and is still on its journey making, I should judge, eight to ten miles per day.

Wm. H. Lentz, 12 Nov 1880

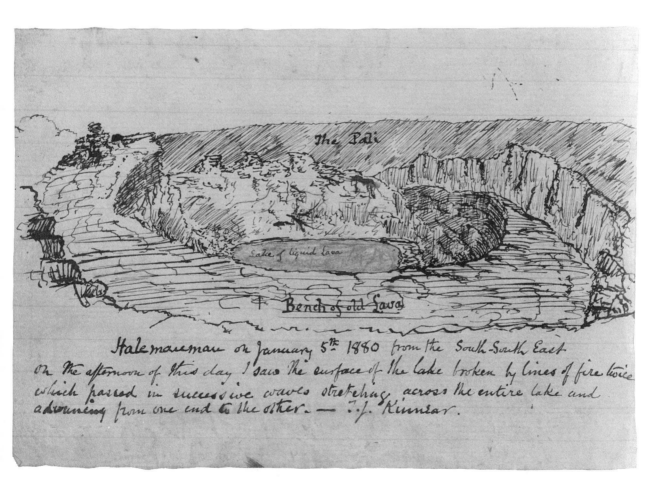

The Pali

Lake of liquid lava

+ Bench of old Lava

Halemaumau on January 5th 1880 from the South-South East
On the afternoon of this day I saw the surface of the lake broken by lines of fire twice which passed in successive waves stretching across the entire lake and advancing from one end to the other. — J.J. Kinnear.

"Hilo Bay" From Waiakea. Mauna Loa in distance — Feb. 1881 —

Joseph Nawahi
Emma A. Nawahi
Miss Mihana Aii.

Resting on the way.

Left Hilo at 9 A.M. on Saturday, February 19th; arrived here at 5:30 P.M. At eight o'clock this evening could be seen the brightening of the lava fire on top of Maunaloa and also in the fire lake of Halemaumau—the new fire lake. February 20th: At 8:30 A.M. made ready to go down to visit the New Lake and to explore the new things of the celebrated home of Madame Pele. Six hours passed in going around the flats of the crater. Saw again this night the incomparably beautiful appearances of brightenings of this place with the fires like lanterns lighting up and staying a while here and there in the crater. In the sketch are the new fire lake and the lakes of Halemaumau and Kilauea close by, and looking at the eruption on Maunaloa. At 10:00 A.M. of this day we are to leave the Home Mauna [*Mountain Home*] to return by way of "the fragrant walls of Puna" [*poetic allusion to Puna*] to arrive again at "the calm of Hanakahi" [*poetic allusion to Hilo*]. We are, with unbounded pleasure in the expressions of aloha of this upland. [*Translated from Hawaiian.*]

Joseph Nawahi, Emma A. Nawahi, Mihana Aii, 21 Feb 1881

The Maunaloa; (Morning) Feb 20th 1881

The New Lake — Feb 20—1881 11.4.11.

In 1882, Captain C. E. Dutton of the United States Geological Survey came to study the volcanoes of Hawaii. A sample of his entries follow, including a discussion of a hypothesized connection between the magma chambers of Mauna Loa and those of Kilauea, an investigation of the 1880–1881 flows of Mauna Loa, and comparisons of the forms of lava on the volcanoes of Hawaii.

The great depression included within the circuit of high walls contains at present two active craters of which the larger and more vigorous one just now is Halemaumau and the other is the so-called "new lake." The caldera has probably been produced by the sinking or subsidence of its platform. Beneath it was a large mass of lava which found vent at some distant point situated at a lower level and drained off—the superincumbent rocks sinking into the cavity thus produced.

It is not probable that the caldera in its full extent was formed suddenly. I should rather suppose that it had been formed gradually, beginning as a pit no larger than Kilauea-iki and gradually enlarging all around its circumference by the successive dropping and sinking of portions of the surrounding wall—here a little, there a little. The "faults" by which the successive slices of walls are detached are well presented to view in numerous places, and the ledges produced by the partially sunken portion are very obvious.

There is an impression upon the minds of many people that in some way a connection exists between the craters of Kilauea and those of Mauna Loa. If it is meant that the lava reservoirs of the two localities are really one and the same, or are connected by a subterranean conduit, the idea seems inadmissible and in violation of the simplest and best known of hydrostatic laws. If such a connection were suddenly established the Kilauea craters would immediately drain the reservoir of Loa down to their own level. If the word "connection" means that the same cause acts upon both and produces eruptions from both, it becomes more intelligible. Such a connection, however, would be proven only by careful and systematic observation kept up during many years. Judging from the rather meager records of past eruptions it appears that disturbances in the craters of Kilauea have in some cases been accompanied by great excitement in Mokuaweoweo. This would seem to show that the cause which sets the one in motion actuates at the same time the other. On the other hand, and more frequently, only one set of craters is disturbed at any one time. This would go to show that the actuating cause generally disturbs the one only, though sometimes it affects both simultaneously.

It is the most forcible illustration to be found in the world that volcanoes do not draw their lavas from an universal and all liquid interior of the earth, but that each volcano has its own independent reservoir of limited or even small extent and entirely disconnected from the reservoirs of other volcanoes even though other volcanoes may be closely adjacent.

Further evidence of the independence of or disconnection of Loa and

Kilauea may be found in the distinct characters of the respective lavas. Those from Loa contain an extraordinary amount of olivine (silica of alumina and magnesia). Those from Kilauea contain but little of that mineral. The quantity of magnetic oxide of iron and of lime-feldspar is greater in the Kilauea than in the Loa lavas. The density of the Kilauea lavas also appears to be somewhat greater — in consequence, no doubt, of the higher percentage of iron.

I have been much interested in watching the action of the lava in the two burning lakes. The phenomenon of a periodical breakout is I think readily explained. The lava is kept liquid by the continuous rise of internal hot steam and other vapors from great depths, sufficient to keep the whole column of lava in fusion. But the quantity of the fresh lava and the heat of the steam thus brought up is insufficient to keep the surface from cooling and forming a semisolid or viscous crust. The crust therefore forms and its temperature falls. The radiation or loss of heat for a time is thereby greatly diminished, and the lava below the crust gains more heat than it loses, and thus grows hotter. Meantime the crust thickens and grows cooler. As it cools its specific gravity increases. As the lava beneath heats up, its specific gravity diminishes, and the ebullition grows more violent. At length the difference in the specific gravities of the crust above and the hot lava below becomes so great that the crust can no longer be sustained. Wherever the ebullition is most violent, there a large breach in the crust is made and it begins to sink. The breakup rapidly extends and in a few minutes the whole crust has gone down. And now for a time the loss of heat by radiation is greater than the accession of heat from below. The descent of the cold crust cools the lava like pieces of ice dropped into warm water. The ebullition diminishes. Soon, however, a new crust forms, checking the radiation and the process repeats itself.

C. E. Dutton, U.S. Ordnance Corps,
Detailed to U.S. Geological Survey, 14 July 1882

On the eighteenth of July I left the Volcano House for the purpose of visiting the source of the great eruption of 1881. The journey was long and in several places rather severe since it was necessary to cross several streams of aa. But the route was selected with admirable judgement by my guide. The Hilo flow is quite distinct from the Kau flow as they plainly came from separate fissures and orifices. Both are near the "divide" and only a quarter of a mile apart. Some of the vents are still fretful and one especially is quite demonstrative, sending out puffs and jets of steam with long and rather irregular pulsations. At another vent we found a small stream of lava which must have been ejected only a very few days before our visit as it was still hot and smoking and quite unsafe to tread upon.

Mokuaweoweo was very quiet. It is a much more impressive caldera than Kilauea being nearly twice as deep and the surrounding cliffs are much more abrupt. This caldera like Kilauea appears to be a recent development in the history of the great mountain and most probably it was formed in the same manner as Kilauea—that is, by the draining of some reservoir beneath its floor and the escape of lava through some orifice upon the flank of the mountain.

C. E. Dutton, U.S. Geol. Survey, July 1882

One very striking feature of Mauna Loa is the great scarcity of cinder cones and the insignificant size of those which do occur. It seems to me that the remarkably flat profile of Mauna Loa may in great part at least be traced to the absence of such fragmental products of eruption. All of the matter extravasated from its many vents being highly liquid lava it flows far away from the vent and distributes itself over great distances.

Very distinct is the portion of the 1881 flow which descended toward Kalaieha. This part of the eruption broke out near the summit and ceased to run when the main flow toward Hilo broke out. Thus the outbreak of last year gave rise to three independent streams—the Kalaieha, the Kau (which is visible from here) and the Hilo streams.

C. E. Dutton, 12 Sept 1882

One of the most prominent features of Kilauea for many years was the "Little Beggar," a small cone whose origin is described here.

In our visit to Madame Pele last night we found a new little crater on the route between Halemaumau. The guide says that it began to form last Tuesday. We visited it as we went to Halemaumau and it looked precisely like the furnace of a blacksmith's forge and not over two feet across but while we were watching Halemaumau the little crater burst forth and gave us a distant view of a lava flow several hundred feet in length. We have named it The Little Beggar on account of its viciousness.

An old gentleman visited the night before, reported that the "*nawsty little beggar* no bigger than your 'ed was spitting away right in our *pawth*, you know, and I had to go so far round to keep away from it that I didn't see the south lake at all." We hope the "Little Beggar" will go on and make a new lake.

C. H. Dickey, Haiku, Maui, 9 March 1884

Went down crater in evening. New Lake broke up while we were present for the first time in several months. Descended to the floor of Halemaumau through the gap on the N. side. The path descends to a point ten to fifteen feet below the level of the lake. The flow from "Little Beggar," which has been running since early in March, has nearly reached the north wall of the crater and is slowly advancing.

L. A. Thurston, 17 May 1885

The cone was a useful landmark.

[101]

On March 6, 1886 the molten lava in Halemaumau Crater drained away. It soon reappeared, and the crater continued refilling until 1891, when, five years later to the day, the lava again disappeared. Meanwhile, Mauna Loa erupted again, in January 1887, along the southwest rift zone.

On the evening of the sixth of March at 7 P.M. both the Old Lake Halemaumau and the New Lake were quite full of boiling and surging lava and very brilliant as seen from the verandah of the House and continued to remain so up to 9:30 P.M. At which time there commenced a series of earthquakes forty-three in number and lasting until 7:30 A.M. Between 2 and 3 A.M. the seventh all fire and lights in the crater had disappeared excepting a few sparks here and there.

For the full months of March and April there was no fire to be seen in crater, only a few cracks where the rocks were red hot. During the latter part of April there commenced to show more signs of the fire returning by the increase of steam and smoke, also the intense heat and the large deposits of sulphur.

no signature, probably J. H. Maby, 7 March 1886

All the burning lava had disappeared. The "little beggar" had practically disappeared, split in two and subsided below the present level of the crater's edge. Mr. Maby tells us that when the Lakes were in existence their surface was several hundred feet above the level of the old lava crust whereon we stood and on the left of the Old Lake high bluffs used to rise and projecting from these was the ledge on which he used to lead tourists to view Halemaumau—all this has been engulfed and it is a mercy no tourists were thereabouts on the sixth inst.

R. E. Finley, Sydney, N.S.W., 10 March 1886

Reappearance of a boiling lava lake in the crater.

no signature, 1 June 1886

The hole that had formed on the night of May the eighth from which issued the first reflection seen from the crater since the disappearance of the fire on the night of March 6th, the hole which was only three or four foot in diameter had increased to about fifty feet.

J. H. Maby, 1 June 1886

The crater is still inactive, only a little fire to be seen.

D. H. Hitchcock, Sept 1886

Had we come a little later
We'd have seen a better crater.

M.P., Sept 1886

After a thorough rest, we spent a charming morning on a visit to Kilauea Iki gathering specimens of the many beautiful mosses along the road; on our return our generous host and hostess served up a splendid lunch. After that of course came the sulphur bath and then the visit to Madame Pele's chief palace. We were grieved to find she had left for a time, having gone evidently to the ones of Mauna Loa which new outbreak we had the unexpected pleasure of seeing on our way up the Kona Coast. It was on the Kona side about two miles from the old flow of '68.

A grand and glorious sight it was—that mass of molten lava pouring down the sides of the grand old mountain a quarter of a mile wide, here and there where it had caught the trees, the flames were very brilliant; the heat was intense even to our steamer.

Hettie Tuck, Honolulu, 22 Jan 1887

Great changes in the crater have been made during the last eleven months, at which time I visited Kilauea with Prof. Dana and party. The great pit formed by the collapse of March 1886 was then over 100 feet below the lava floor of the crater at that point, in the center of which was the great cone; this pit is now essentially filled.

W. C. Merritt, 14 July 1888

Open lake again.

J. H. Maby, 16 Sept 1890

Lake Halemaumau was not quite so active as reported the night before. Yet the dark lava crust showed fire cracks in many places, with frequent ebullitions and outpourings of a molten mass. One place, in particular, near the northeastern quarter, maintained a steady flow. Our guides went right down to the verge of the lake, thrust their sticks through the piecrust on top, pulled out little masses as do glass burners from their furnaces, and placed in them sundry coins as a curiosity. Near us the lake maintained a constant series of puffing explosions as if of pent-up steam, but from any point made by us it was not practicable to observe their real nature. The cones in the lake displayed fine pyrotechnics of lava jets and balls, with but slight interruption.

Starting on toward Dana Lake we soon reached what Mr. Peck called Le Conte Lake, which the night before had been one molten sea. It was more quiet under our first view but immediately began to perform, a center of surging fire appearing from which a molten rim rapidly expanded until the whole area was brilliantly covered.

Dana Lake maintained its eminent reputation, the entire mass, surface and depth, boiling violently, and throwing up spouts and bombs of fire. The guide said the surface was about 200 feet long and 100 wide. But we discovered that what seemed its shore was not a shore, but only a shelf or floor under which the fiery molten caverns extended an unknown distance. At times the mass of tempestuous, boiling lava seemed impelled by a rapid current to the western end, and pouring out of sight into an invisible vortex.

A very striking feature, which the guide pronounced new, appeared some distance perhaps south from Dana Lake. An active eruption, apparently on the crater's rim, probably a third or halfway toward the top, poured out a liquid, fiery mass which flowed in a tortuous stream downward toward the center of the crater. Its flow and figure made a veritable river of fire.

Chauncey N. Pond, Oberlin, Ohio, 11 Oct 1890

James D. Dana.

Explored floor of crater. "New Lake" resembles an irregular bowl of seventy-five feet diameter, sides six to ten feet high. Lava inside at white heat, surging, boiling, bubbling, sputtering, swashing and dashing itself against the sides, sometimes slopping over.

"Dana Lake" is similar, say four times as large, with higher walls and boiling with more intense fury. There were fifteen or twenty blow holes scattered about us, all seeming to open into a turbulent subterranean river; out of some the lava was shot with great velocity, high into the air.

Others breathed a blue flame with regular pulsations of sound louder than that from the valve of any engine of man's making. The solid lava trembling with the throes of the monster confined within.

George A. Howard, Los Angeles, 3 Jan 1891

On the morning of the eighth on looking over the crater we saw that the cones at Halemaumau, the Dana, and Maby Lake had sunk out of sight.

It being just five years to a day between the time of the bottom dropping out on March 6, 1886 and the present drop out.

J. H. Maby, 6 March 1891

About 11 P.M. this day the fire returned in the sunken pit of Halemaumau, after having been extinguished thirty-five days. When first inspected on the eleventh of April, the fire was very small, occupying or puffing out of a small hole at the bottom, not more than four or five feet in diameter.

H. M. Whitney, 10 April 1891

The molten lava has greatly risen within four months. In May last the liquid fire was four or 500 feet below the surface or brink of the chasm, it is now up about 200 feet below. The molten material is sufficiently hot to keep the crust on the surface of the lake steadily viscid, and bearing about the same relation to the liquid mass below, which cream bears to the milk in a pan which it covers.

Edwd. P. Baker, 14 Sept 1891

In 1892, Mokuaweoweo again erupted.

The crater of Mokuaweoweo again active, after a quiet rest of pretty near six years, since February 1887. The fire appeared last night between 10 and 11 o'clock, quietly rising from the summit of Mauna Loa without any earthquakes or previous signs of disturbance, and continued all night. This morning great columns of smoke are belching forth.

The crater of Kilauea continues in its usual activity not seeming in the least affected by the eruption on Mauna Loa.

The fire only lasted three days.

Peter Lee, manager Volcano House, 1 Dec 1892

The fire is now entirely confined to the great South Lake. Should the S. Lake fill up more, it is probable that a large lake will be formed in the centre, which if it does take place will most likely cause the whole centre of Kilauea to subside and again form what in "Auld lang syne" was called the "black ledge."

D. H. Hitchcock, 6 Nov 1868

The centre of the crater appears to be sinking more, at each visit I make, and will (as it now is below the level of the fires in the South Lake) sooner or later break out. The inner ledge, or Black Ledge of the "Ancients" is becoming more and more well defined.

D. H. Hitchcock, 10 Jan 1870

The Black Ledge is formed by overflows from the Lake. Mr. Lee states that about two months ago the surface of the molten lava sank about 150 feet below the level of the Black Ledge. After remaining at that level for about one month it began rising again, and is now within twenty-five feet of its original level.

L. A. Thurston, 12 Feb 1892

Almost daily overflows have taken place. The "black ledge" is being thus built up at the rate of several inches per week.

A. B. Lyons, 13 July 1892

Most of the Black Ledge is extremely hot to walk on. Red hot lava visible through cracks only a few inches below surface. The aspect of the Black Ledge is changing constantly; where it one day was a smooth flat surface, next day will be found a big hill thirty feet high and 100 feet long; as this hill cools off it will crack on top to the extent of two–three feet wide with a tremendous burst. Through this crack the hot lava will force its way in big streams till the surroundings for several hundred feet have been filled up to the level of top of the hill. The rising of the Black Ledge is due more to this action than to overflows from the Lake.

no signature, 1 Feb 1893

One of the distinctive features of Kilauea was a rim of lava that formed when molten lava in the lake would rise, cool, and harden along its edge. When the lava level dropped down again, the cooled lava rim would be left behind. This ledge came to be referred to as the Black Ledge. Five entries describe the status of the Black Ledge over several years.

[107]

Visitors noticed the constant position of certain features, including the location of the molten lake and a prominent lava fountain called "Old Faithful," whose ebullitions were regular like those of the famous geyser in Yellowstone.

The descriptions of the crater of Kilauea, all the rough plans in the Volcano House books, and the plats and maps drawn to scale by actual measurement agree in this, that the lake of lava is fixed in one and the same position, that is in the southwest section of the floor. After every disappearance of molten lava it reappears in the same relative place — there or thereabouts — That Spot is Halemaumau.

W. Goodale, Dec 1893

The lake was active, the largest fountain (Old Faithful) playing once or twice a minute, coming up each time as one, two or three large bubbles and then being quiet till the next burst, the other fountains, four to six generally at a time playing often several minutes before quieting down. Old Faithful always played in the same place in which it played in March 1892 when I saw it on four different days. The guide says it has been in the same place ever since. The other fountains were not confined to any particular locality.

W. F. Frear, 7 Aug 1894

In December 1894, the lava lake drained away again, and all was quiet, with only occasional glimpses of molten lava, until 1907.

The fire in the Crater disappeared quietly during the night, December 6, 1894.

J.M.L. [*Jens Martin Lee, brother of Peter Lee*], *no date*

The lava returned to the crater January 3rd 1896 at 11:30 P.M. and formed during that night the lake. There has been no fire in the crater since December 6, 1894. A longer period of inactivity than any previously recorded.

J. M. Lee, 3 Jan 1896

The fire disappeared again on January 28, 1896.

J. M. Lee, 28 Jan 1896

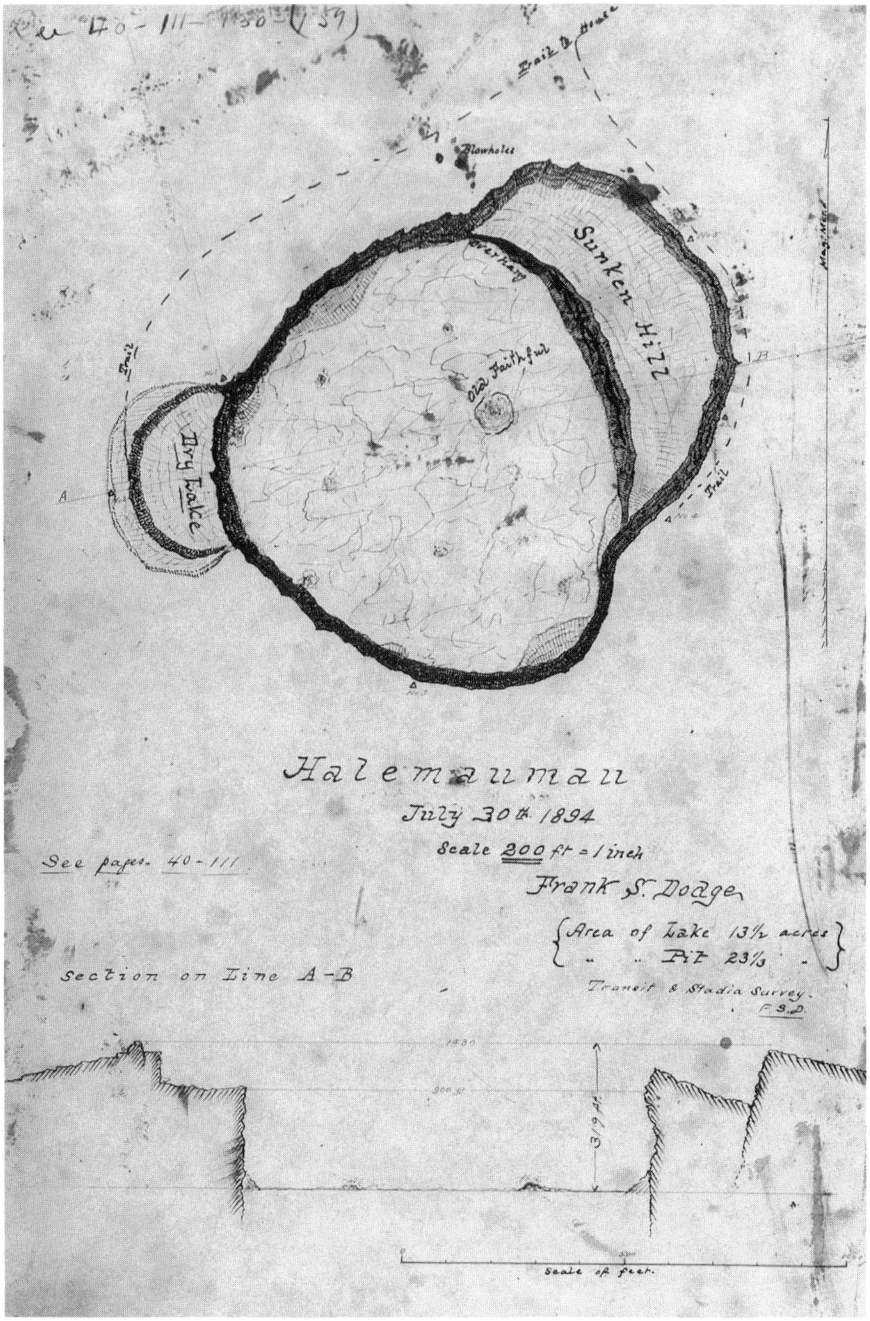

Trail to House
Blowholes
Sunken Hill
Overhang
Old Faithful
Dry Lake
Trail
Trail
A
B
Halemaumau
July 30th 1894
Scale 200 ft = 1 inch
Frank S. Dodge
See pages 40-111
Area of Lake 13½ acres
" " Pit 23⅓ "
Section on Line A-B
Transit & Stadia Survey.
F.S.D.
319 ft
Scale of feet.

Kilauea is continuously smoking but no lava to be seen.

Peter Lee, 6 May 1896

Kilauea active again! Fire returned July 11th.

J. M. Lee, 22 July 1896

The activity continued for three weeks. After this the lava-lake gradually disappeared and the fire was confined to a cone in the bottom from which the lava occasionally poured out. This kept on during August and September when the last sign of fire disappeared.

On June 24th there was again a little fire visible. No lake was formed and no molten lava was seen. The fire was way down in a deep hole or cave in the bottom, and only the reflection against the sides of the cave could be seen. The fire this time lasted three days only. For several months back the smoke has been very dense and voluminous.

J. M. Lee, 24–26 June 1897

VOLCANIC ACTIVITY

The crater of Mokuaweoweo is again active. The fire broke out some time during last night, but on account of dense clouds enveloping Mauna Loa the smoke was not noticed from here till 7:25 this morning. At intervals when the clouds roll by we can see the fire brilliantly reflected in the sky.

J. M. Lee, 21 April 1896

The crater of Mokuaweoweo is the grandest sight my eyes ever beheld seen as we saw it—the lake of fire, the great fountains playing continuously, one of them throwing up a mighty column of orange colored flame to a height of 250 feet. Such a trip is the crowning experience of a lifetime.

Kilauea—Halemaumau—is quiescent, Madam Pele having apparently removed her royal court to the summit of Mt. Loa which has put on white in honor of her presence.

Elbert R. Dille, Pastor Central M.E. Church
San Francisco, 1 May 1896

Tuesday, April 28, 1896, an expedition left the Volcano House for the crater of Mokuaweoweo, on the summit of Mauna Loa, which had been in eruption about eleven days. The camping place for the night, Kepukakina, is reached at 3 P.M. The reflection of the volcano more than five thousand feet above, upon great banks of moonlit clouds rolling over the crest of the mountain is in itself worth the trouble of the trip. Besides this a sunrise unparalleled in gorgeousness, a golden landscape laved with a royal purple sea. At an elevation of 9600 feet, a cloud sweeps along the face of the mountain. It carries snow and hail alternately, a regular down-easterly pelting snowstorm; the sensation produced by this one was not disagreeable but rather exhilarating. Most of the remainder of the journey is over precipitous ridges. The trail winds zigzaggedly amongst a wilderness of hills made of every variety of lava. At length we actually meet the horizon. This is the first time I have ever seen a veritable jumping off place. For here we come to a stone parapet and, looking beyond it, while standing on its outer verge, we see nothing ahead but sheer atmosphere adulterated with drifting snow. There is indeed the flame of an enormous candle in the midst of the white oblivion. It is a light shining in white darkness, and the advance riders swing their hats and cheer. This is the volcano. The exercise of riding being past, the excursionists are soon shivering violently in the pitiless blast, against which there is not even the shadow of a barricade. There is a cleft in the rocks, however, provided by some benevolent earthquake long ago. It is not more than two yards

Meanwhile, Mokuaweoweo had a spectacular eruption during the months of April and May, 1896.

[111]

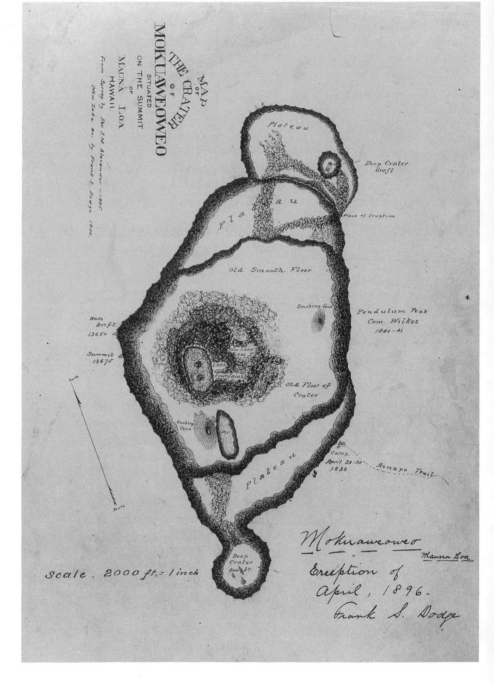

MAP
OF
THE CRATER
OF
MOKUAWEOWEO
SITUATED
ON THE SUMMIT
OF
MAUNA LOA
HAWAII.
From Survey by Rev. J.M. Alexander - 1885
New Lake &c. by Frank S. Dodge 1896.

Plateau

Deep Crater
600 ft

Plateau

Place of Eruption

Old Smooth Floor

Smoking Cone

Pendulum Peak
Com. Wilkes
1840-41

Walls
800 ft.
13650

Summit
13675

New Lava
1896

Lake
and
Fountains

Old Floor of
Crater

North

Smoking
Cone

Pit

Plateau

Camp.
April 25-30
1896

Ainapo Trail

South

Deep
Crater
800 ft.

Scale, 2000 ft = 1 inch

Mokuaweoweo
Mauna Loa
Eruption of
April, 1896.
Frank S. Dodge

from the brink of the crater, and into it we huddle while we anxiously await the raising of the curtain for the exhibition of the wonder we have mounted the stately dome to see. As if to introduce us by degrees to a spectacle too stupendous for surprising mortal eyes in one instant, the swirling tempest from the skies gradually abates within the crater. For a few minutes even the candle already mentioned becomes hidden. It suddenly flares up again and as we strain our gaze it is transformed into a sputtering fountain of exploding rockets, whose fiery trail is seen all at once. Then another flame appears away to the left, not rising high but burning fiercely like the fire excited in a forge by the bellows. At the same time the screen parts two or three hundred feet to the right, disclosing another fountain of only less magnitude than the first. Continuing to dissipate, the shimmering white veil is at last totally vanished, leaving the entire crater of Mokuaweoweo exposed to view in a clear atmosphere. If there is a word better than sublime to describe awful grandeur and gorgeous beauty in combination, the reader must be left to supply it. The fountains of Mokuaweoweo are different from those of Kilauea when in activity, in that they preserve their relative positions toward each other and their environment, besides being in constant and uniform action. In the lake of Halemaumau in the Kilauea crater, on the other hand, the fountains are constantly changing in position and number both, and sometimes for several minutes the entire surface would be crusted over, showing scarcely a streak of fire. The forms assumed by the fountains of Mokuaweoweo are of exceeding beauty. Each one shows a multiplied facade of spires composed of thousands of bunched jets of orange color. The whole effect is that of an illuminated Gothic cathedral front. There is a steady aa flow from the fierce caldrons, which is fast covering a deposit of pahoehoe that we generally agree came from a former eruption. We see its outer edge being pushed slowly but surely by the grinding and rolling mass. The heat produces a fierce whirlwind at the opposite side of the crater. It is slender and pale brown, high as the cliff opposite, or a thousand feet, and symmetrical as a Corinthian pillar. As it rushes along at galloping speed, with a spiral motion, its lower end rips up the massive lava crust in huge slabs and tosses these aside like the action of a steamer's propeller in friable ice. There is an exposure of fire beneath at every upturning of the crust. Human endurance has its limit, however, and, with few exceptions, when the party, in two tents, wrapped their blankets around them over an unusually thick covering of outer clothing, and lay down in huddled ranks to invoke "his beloved sleep" upon the stone mattress, there was no arising until at dawn the call to breakfast and saddle was made. Mr. Hitchcock made sketches in colors of both day and night displays, and we are confident that the results will be worthy records in art of the Mokuaweoweo eruption of 1896.

Daniel Logan, 2 May 1896

First Party To Mokuaweoweo

The above party left the Volcano House at 8:30 A.M. July 21 enroute to the crater. Instead of following the long trail through the koa grove and up the flow of 1881, they travelled directly towards the crater. Camp was made near the Red Hills. The sight was grand. Words were utterly insufficient. The lava red hot came pouring over a precipice, into the channel below. We estimated the width at thirty feet, depth fifteen, speed, twenty miles per hour. Naming the Crater. After a restless night spent on the hot lava we arose at daybreak and after a light breakfast we unfurled two American flags, each bearing the inscription "The Wilson Party deposited this flag and christened this cone Admiral Dewey on July 22 1899." The flags were placed in position. Hereafter the crater would be known as "Admiral Dewey."

Wilson Party, 23 July 1899

In 1899 Mauna Loa erupted both at its summit and along the northeast rift zone; the rift activity included the formation of Dewey Cone. The next eruption of Mauna Loa was in late 1903, and lasted for about two months.

October 6, 1903. The summit crater Mokuaweoweo broke out today at 12:45 P.M. without any warning—no earthquakes or reports but a very large column of smoke shot up many hundreds of feet and spread out like an immense umbrella, and continued so until dark, when what had been a column of smoke by day, was truly a "pillar of fire by night." The sight from the Volcano House was enjoyed by quite a few guests who were fortunate in being here at the time.

Dec 8, 1903 10 P.M. Activity ceased in Mokuaweoweo.

St. Claire Bidgood, Mgr. Volcano House, *no date*

Halemaumau remained quiet for nearly a year, with only a rare glow visible from the lava.

Tuesday night about ten o'clock was wakened by Mrs. Waldron and for about an hour and a half watched a glowing over Halemaumau both from the upper rooms at the house and later from the observation point on the bluff. Saw the glowing distinctly and could locate it as coming from a puka some distance down the Kau side.

Herbert S. Griggs, Tacoma, Washington, 8 June 1902

[114]

1903 Outbreak of Mokuaweoweo

Thos. C. Ridgway

Halemaumau is active again! A glow was seen above the crater at 4:15 A.M. On going down we found a lake had formed about 40 x 125 feet in the bottom of crater. Fountains were playing continually.

no signature, but probably St. Claire Bidgood, 25 Nov 1903

Halemaumau remained active until January 10th, 1904.

Fire Appears Again. One week ago today, on a visit to the crater we saw the first fire that had been observed in the pit for about a year. The glow was plainly visible from the Volcano House.

George Henshall, 9 Dec 1906

Mauna Loa's outbreak of 1907 was first noticed at about 11:30 on Wednesday evening, January 8. It was seen in Hilo at that time and by twelve midnight a great illumination of the clouds above the mountain caused a general awakening of the residents of the town. The observers saw a wide column, almost of fire as it appeared reaching up to clouds which were colored as by a red sunset.

On Saturday telephone messages from Kona and Kau told of lava flows, confirming earlier reports of a flow started towards Kona and possibly hidden in the clouds till it reached lower levels.

Today, Sunday, January 13, it is definitely reported that the flow has reached and crossed the government road in Kau. Kilauea has continued, as on other occasions, apparently unaffected by the vast activity of her parent mountain.

George P. Henshall, 13 Jan 1907

In 1907 Mauna Loa erupted on the southwest rift zone, producing a lava flow that lasted about two weeks.

Molten lava returned to Halemaumau as well in 1907, and the lake was almost continually active until 1924—except for minor episodes of draining in 1916, 1919, 1922, and 1923. During the 1907–1924 period, many visitors recorded descriptions of the activity, some comparing present activity with that of former days, others analyzing the mechanisms operating in the lava lake.

The volcano became active again today after a quietness of about seven months. Miss Hattie Hitchcock was the first one saw the glow from the Volcano House at 9 P.M. and drew everybody's attention to it. The whole of Halemaumau was lit up thus made it look very brilliant from the house.

D. Lycurgus, 30 Nov 1907

I visited the crater. The scene was very different to that presented on my previous visit (December 1905). At that time the lava was about 600 feet below the brink and scarcely alive, fire being sometimes visible through the thick smoke, but never to any extent. Today, the lava has risen to probably less than 150 feet from the top and is in constant motion throughout most of the mass.

G. W. Kirkaldy, Honolulu, 18 April 1908

The finest sight I ever witnessed. Top of the cone blew off last night and display was wonderful.

E. S. Aldrich, Moscow, Idaho, 24 April 1908

Made a third trip to the lake of fire for this month. It is increasing in size, now some twenty acres of molten fire. The pit of Halemaumau is slowly but steadily filling up.

Edward W. Thwing, 23 June 1908

One may obtain a graphic idea of the profile of this fire-lake, its enclosing border of pahoehoe, and the enclosing pit walls against which the latter abuts, by imagining a huge dinner-plate turned upside down; this dinner plate surrounded by a hoop applied to its rim. The hoop will then represent the vertical wall of the pit. The sloping border of the plate will represent the pahoehoe that surrounds the fire-lake; and the flat bottom of the plate with its encircling bead the fire-lake and its low rim.

A, B = Vertical walls of the pit.
C, D = Surrounding border of black pahoehoe.
E = Fire-lake.

Fire-fountains. One in particular has been so constant as to receive the name "Old Faithful." The action of "O.F." is not continuous. He takes a rest every few minutes and allows small scales of relatively black lava to form over him. After a short period of inactivity and scaling-over, of a sudden there is a jet of red lava within the circle of his action: the lava-scales begin to tilt on edge and to be sucked down into vortices; then, in an instant, the surface of the pot swells up in one huge, rotund, white-hot mass, leaping high into the air. This action continues for many seconds or a minute, and presently subsides.

N. B. Emerson, 18 Aug 1908

I suggest, as a subject for further investigation and consideration, that, as a matter of fact, the lava is not flowing off thru or under the bank; but simply strikes the bank, goes downward, and comes up again at the central uprising spot—creating a continuous current. When the molten lava in the pit is drained off, as it has been a number of times, leaving the banks exposed to some hundreds of feet, no caverns have been revealed.

The "fountain" is not throwing up a fresh supply of lava, but consists simply of a discharge of gas, which, instead of being continuous, comes up in great bubbles, which as they rise from the great depths, must be under great pressure. As they near the surface the pressure rapidly decreases, in consequence of which the bubbles expand, finally reaching the surface with sufficient expansive energy to drive the surrounding lava up ahead of it in a fiery spray, or "fountain." As no new lava has arrived, there is none to flow away—hence no current *away* from the fountain.

If the above suggestion that the fountain consists of gas and not new lava, is correct, it would then follow that the rapid expulsion of a large quantity of gas must leave a considerable empty space or vacuum, especially near the surface, where relief from pressure would result in great expansion. As the expanded gas bursts thru and from the lava, the adjacent lava would rush in to fill the vacancy, causing a current toward the point of activity.

L. A. Thurston, 6 May 1909

Sketch of Halemaumau Dec. 21st 1908.

Nearly all the old-time descriptions tell of cones and fountains—usually two or three—and relate with enthusiasm how the black area was streaked with red and at intervals broken up. The lava is too liquid now for cones to be a possibility and it would be impossible to count the number of fountains playing at once. What patches of black there are, are but floating spots which are easily seen to be areas of a very thin film above the fire and none of them last any length of time.

A party visiting the crater yesterday morning witnessed a splendid "storm" on the fiery lake. Two opposing waves of lava met in a line across the center and as the two masses of molten matter clashed, there was a boiling and roaring like the agitation of violently boiling water. An idea of the fury of these storms on the lake of fire may be gained from the fact that when the air is still, the roar of the infernal surf is distinctly audible at the Volcano House.

During such angry outbursts great quantities of "Pele's hair" are formed. It may be seen rising from the fire and the wind is piling a great deal of it on the south side of the pit.

George P. Henshall, 1 Dec 1909

W. Grayling. Temple.

I wrote in the Volcano House Book Oct 11, 1890 the condition of the crater then. The contrasts are very impressive.

1. There is now only one lake of fire instead of two before, or three according as they were classified.
2. The difference of level is very great. The lava on fire is now down probably 175 feet, whereas in 1890 I saw Halemaumau so close to the top that the guides, and some of the party, went down and put their sticks into the fire and pulled out little chunks of viscid lava.
3. There are now no cones at all in the active crater and they, the cones, were very prominent then.
4. There is now no area that is constantly boiling in one incessant lake of fire as did Dana Lake then.

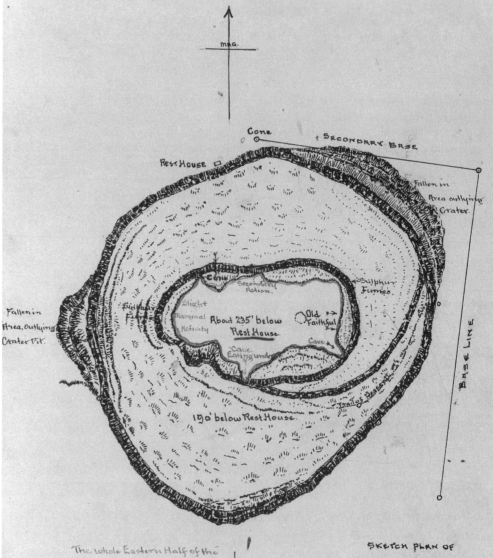

mag.

Cone   ↑ SECONDARY BASE

REST HOUSE ☐

Fallen in
Area outlying
Crater.

Cone
Secondary
Action.

Sulphur
Fumes

Slight
Marginal
Activity

About 235' below
Rest House.

Old
Faithful

Sulphur
Fumes

Cave
Eating under

Cave.

BASE LINE

150' below Rest House.

Trailed Deposit

Fallen in
Area, outlying
Crater Pit.

The whole Eastern Half of the
Lake is in a state of continuous
Activity with Old Faithful playing
10' to 20' every 35 to 45 Seconds

SKETCH PLAN OF

HALEMAUMAU

SCALE 300:1"

JULY 1909   J.M.Lydgate.

The present characteristics are as follows:

1. A pit perhaps 500 feet in diameter.
2. A ledge down all around that pit, perhaps seventy-five feet down, and seventy-five feet wide all around the pit.
3. A deeper pit below that ledge, full of the lava, all around, but perhaps 100 feet down below the ledge.
4. This deeper pit is the scene of the active crater. The mass is aglow with intense heat.
5. The surface, in patches of fluid fire and viscid lava, moved inward from the north and south edges toward some middle line where the masses seemed to be swallowed up as by an invisible, straight lined vortex, and yet the level was not depressed.
6. "Old Faithful" as one particular spot was called, kept throwing up ebullitions of glowing lava.

Chauncey N. Pond, Oberlin, O., 3 March 1910

An observatory should be established here as soon as possible.

M. Horner, England, 21 Oct 1890

I cannot but think that the Congress of this great and rich Republic, would certainly, the matter being properly represented, supply means to keep an educated scientist to observe and record the various wonderful natural phenomena of the locality of Hawaii's great volcano, the most accessible in the world.

Charles F. Hart, 20 Feb 1907

There is one thing which it seems to me should have been done long ago and that is: there should have been established here some facilities for the scientific study of the volcano and for the preservation of an accurate record of the frequent changes which have been occurring in one of the world's greatest wonders. It is to be hoped that some provision may be made in the not distant future so that further changes may be noted and a reliable history may be kept of this marvelous manifestation of nature.

Charles W. Fairbanks [*Vice-president of the United States*], 6 May 1909

Many visitors realized that, as delightful as the Volcano House Register was, something more was needed for keeping a record of volcanic activity: an observatory.

This crater has more than spectacular significance. It presents an unique opportunity for the study of scientific phenomena. Mankind has always been prostrate while eruptions have snuffed out countless lives and laid waste cities and lands. The hand of man can never restrain these outbreaks but by a proper study of habits and symptoms the disturbances may be predicted and the people thereby prepared for flight. Now we are ignorant, having little or no acquaintance with the significant facts and conditions that would enable this man on guard to predict. Therefore let everyone know, appreciate and support the plans recently made to establish a seismological laboratory on the brink of the fire pit. The scope of the proposed study will be broader than the prediction of eruptions, but this feature alone makes it well worthy of the nation's support and maintenance.

M. O. Leighton, Washington D.C., 6 Sept 1909

Made a visit to Kilauea-iki and took several altitudes with an aneroid. For the benefit of those who wish to know I'll give a summary of my results:

Depth of Kilauea-iki below north bank, 750 ft.
Depth of Kilauea-iki below Kilauea, 380 ft.
Dimensions of Kilauea-iki 1800 x 1400 ft.
Top of north bank of Kilauea-iki below Volcano H. 120ft.
Kilauea-iki below Vol. H. 870 ft.

I found, by my aneroid, when I returned, that in some unaccountable manner, the Volcano House had, during my absence, risen twenty feet. This piece of tomfoolery on the part of Dame Nature while my back was turned, I'm wholly at a loss to account for.

M. C. Mott-Smith, 24 June 1899

On April 4, 1909 temperatures of the steam from the sulphur banks W. of hotel, measured with Bristol portable pyrometer (thermo-couple and milli-voltmeter with two special scales reading to 400 and 1200 Centigrade respectively) gave readings from 30 to 105 C, the smaller fissures giving the higher temperatures. Some of these show considerable superheat and various forms of sulphur are deposited on the most highly heated surfaces.

On April 5, the temperatures of vapor vents on trail from edge of Crater of Kilauea across the pa-hoe-hoe lava to Halemaumau were 95, 84, 93, 92,

67, 85 C. Intense superheat was found in the large steaming solfataric area about 250 yards north of the edge of Halemaumau: here the readings in small one-inch fissures lined with sulphur were 166 C, 178 C. In this same area, on April 6th, near where the largest jet of vapor is seen from the Hotel, a temperature of 300 C was obtained. That this is not a rock temperature independent of water, occasioned by hot lava immediately beneath, is proved by the presence of dense clouds of water vapor almost wholly free from the odor of sulphur, and by the absence of such sulphur fumes as would be occasioned by the roasting action of hot lava on older lava. The rocks are intensely cracked and whitened by the superheated water vapor. There is no sign of the roasting of sulphides to produce blue fumes of SO_2 such as are abundantly seen in the older rocks adjacent to the lake of fluid basalt in the crater. In making these temperature measurements the writer was assisted by Mrs. Jaggar and Mr. J. J. Kline.

T. A. Jaggar Jr., Boston, Mass., 7 April 1909

Besides tourists, various scientists visited Kilauea in the early twentieth century to make observations and conduct experiments. These included T. A. Jaggar, F. A. Perret, and E. S. Shepherd. Dr. Jaggar immediately saw the need for careful observations and records of changes at the volcano. He returned to Hawaii in 1912 to set up the Hawaiian Volcano Observatory. These entries describe some of the early experiments and observations by men of science.

I have been here over three weeks at intervals during the last month. The place grows upon me and the volcano increases in interest. It is so different from anything I have seen in the Old World, the West Indies or in Central America. There one sees volcanoes building up piles of ashes and lava by explosion and outflow. Here explosion is subordinated, while there goes on also a process of solution and undermining which at present is more active than the building up. This is really the most striking difference noticeable.

Beyond this the steadiness and restrained activity of Kilauea is remarkable. In regularity Stromboli in Europe compares, but in its case activity takes the form of frequent small explosions instead of a steady flow. The volcano I have seen most strictly comparable is Matavanu that broke out in 1905 in Savaii near Samoa. In that case a river of molten lava flows in the bottom of the crater, enters a tunnel, and runs underground several miles to the sea, into which it flows visibly by many changing mouths with formation of vast clouds of steam. Matavanu therefore is certainly a river, while Kilauea may be either a river or a boiling pot.

Characteristic of this whole region, and unknown to me elsewhere are the pit craters so frequent here of which Kilauea and the crater of Mauna Loa are prominent examples.

Tempest Anderson, Stonegate, York, England, 11 July 1909

An expedition from Mass. Inst. Tech. and consisting of L. A. Perret of the Volcanic Research Society and E. S. Shepherd of the Geophysical Laboratory Carnegie Inst. of Wash. after a month's work in stretching and adjusting cables this day succeeded in lowering a pyrometer into Old Faithful and obtaining a temperature reading of 1010 Centigrade (1850 F) for the lava about two feet below the crust. The fountains are perhaps one or at times two hundred degrees (C) hotter, but no system yet devised will stand the mechanical strain combined with the heat and chemical action, which these fountains produce. Two pyrometers were lost by being jerked down by the inrush of lava which follows the upheaval of the fountains.

Here's hoping that a permanent observatory will be one of the results of this effort at a quantitative study of this splendid volcano.

E.S.S., 31 July 1911

Eight to 9 P.M. tonight the lava pool could be seen clearly from the eastern A-frame. The pool appeared to be about 350 feet down and was boiling vigorously. There was a glowing spot south of the pool and a glowing group of cavities with flames east of it. A great vortex carried the fumes in a circular path from the talus on the south side northward along the talus bench then up the wall, up, and in a broad sweep downward again to the south. The pool could be seen through this eddy as though through a circular window. There was little to be seen from other places. There were few slides heard and little blowing but the lava was splashing noisily.

T. A. Jaggar Jr., 13 Sept 1912

The trail to the new crater completed, Mr. Lycurgus and I were the first to ride over it, and I had the honor of naming the crater Puhi Mau (Always Steaming).

Sara R. Dougherty, 5 Nov 1910

As access improved, people were also becoming interested in the geomorphology of Kilauea in areas beyond Halemaumau.

First visit 1882. Second 1887. Third 1889. Several times since. Have seen it better perhaps but was too young to appreciate it. We today renamed the old Devil's Throat "Omolemoo" or Fafner's Flagon after measuring it roughly. It will so be entered in the "Official Map" by Professors J. and W.

J. A. Wilder, 5 Aug 1912

Something like this Billiard Bottle shaped and about 200 feet deep. Opening about 50 feet. Worth seeing! Three or four miles from the road.

In 1912 the Hawaiian Volcano Observatory was established under the directorship of T. A. Jaggar, assisted by H. O. Wood. Subsequently, visitors' comments frequently revolved around these scientists and the need to aid the observatory. Dr. Jaggar also continued to occasionally write in the Register.

A suddenly increased brilliance in the fume cloud over the crater at eight o'clock last night attracted the attention of everyone in the hotel and the big auto bus took a large party down. At first the whole crater was obscured by fumes and there was disappointment in the party, especially as Dr. Jaggar stated that there had been a splendid flow from the northeast cone at 8 P.M. But at 10 P.M. from the South East Station our party had a fine view of the whole floor, and a new flow started from the west end which spread in a few moments over nearly half the floor. Old Faithful meanwhile was very active, and a new pool nearly as large as Old Faithful was continuously and furiously active, so that all the heavens were lighted with the glow. It was the finest display for some weeks.

Wade Warren Thayer, 15 July 1914

My sixth visit. We took in the Tree Molds, The Fern Forest, The Sulphur Banks, The Observatory (under the intensely interesting and instructive guidance of Professor Jaggert) Thurston's Cave, Kilauea Iki, and Halemaumau. Everything proved most enjoyable. The crater was very active.

William A. Bowen, Honolulu, 13 Nov 1914

We left Honolulu on the evening of the twelfth for the very first steamer Matsonia. Came on to the Volcano House—saw the sulphur beds the tree molds—Fern Forests—and the U.S. Observatory—under the very efficient care of Professor Jaggert.

L. H. Kennedy and wife, Rockport, Ind., 14 Nov 1914

A great mystery that deserves the active aid from the Federal Govt. in order to aid scientific investigation.

Jas. Frear, Wis., *no date*

During our stay here we visited the Observatory and through the kindness of Prof. H.O. Wood were shown the Seismographs and some very interesting maps and photographs of earthquakes which have taken place in different localities from time to time.

James McLean, 27 May 1915

Measurements on the 19th October reveal the extraordinary fact that during the preceding six days the lake rose thirty feet without overflowing at all, the great ledges rising with it. The present depression of the lake surface is 243 feet below the south rim of the pit. The large northern crag mass in the lake is sixty feet above the lava, and the ledges northeast and southwest are forty feet above the lava. The lake is 775 feet long in a direction NNW-SSE and 625 feet wide at the widest part. The floor of the pit is 1125 feet across. The inner bench immediately over the lake is fourteen feet high.

This rising of the ledges does not mean that they floated up, but that lava wedged in below them and solidified, intruding among them, breaking and lifting them.

T.A.J., Jr., 20 Oct 1916

After an all-night's vigil alone watching the ever-changing phenomena of Pele's Boiling Cauldron, I find that no poor words of mine can describe the mingled feelings of reverence and admiration with which Kilauea inspires me. If I ever came near disobeying a Scriptural injunction against envy it is now: I am filled with envy of Professor Jaggar and Wood.

signature illegible, 2 March 1917

Six visitors from Submarine Division Fourteen whose trip was made most instructive due to the kindness of Professor and Mrs. Jaggar.

C. E. Frank, 18 Jan 1920

Made our second visit to volcano. Find it very active but very much changed. Today we visited the outbreak of lava in the Kau Desert. That is almost as wonderful.

Mr. and Mrs. C. A. Pratt, Tacoma, Wn., 29 Jan 1920

The first to see Mme. Pele in action on this morning at 12:10 a.m. from Volcano House window. We'll get up at midnight for a "Paul Revere" ride any time for an experience of this kind.

Mr. and Mrs. J. J. Schumacher, Los Angeles, Cal.,
20 Feb 1929

Wakened at one o'clock by cry "Volcano active" by whistles and by an attempt to blow bugle. Flame shot smoke and steam rising from Halemaumau. Five mile drive to edge of pit. Roar like gigantic oil burner. From cracks at least 1000 feet in length bubbling spouting liquid flame spurted. At eastern end fountain at least 150 ft. high. Lava gradually filling bottom of crater. Great experience.

Alice Pattison Merritt, Hartford, Connecticut, 20 Feb 1929

In 1919 the lava level in Halemaumau dropped, and Kilauea erupted in the Kau Desert on the southwest rift zone. This eruption continued into 1920, and eventually formed the small shield volcano Mauna Iki.

In the spring of 1924, major changes occurred at Kilauea: earthquakes caused subsidence of the land in Puna, and the lava in Halemaumau lake subsequently drained away. Water came in contact with the magma underground, resulting in phreatic explosions — violent steam explosions that ejected already-cooled rock, rather than molten lava, from Halemaumau Crater. Huge boulders were hurled out, and giant cauliflower-shaped steam clouds repeatedly rose above the crater.

The diameter of Halemaumau Crater roughly doubled during this period, as the pit collapsed over the void created by the removal of magma, which may have fed an undersea eruption along the east rift zone.

There is no record of these activities in the Volcano House Register, because the volume covering the years 1923–1926 is missing.

Following the 1924 explosion, there was a ten-year period of quiescence, during which activity was only intermittent. There were eruptions in February and July of 1929, and brief eruptions in 1930, 1931, and 1934. But the continuous lava lake was gone.

We rushed madly over from Honolulu to view the sudden fury of Madam Pele, to find her anger somewhat subsided — but are thrilled to see the great cracks of fiery lava and the boiling seething mass in the center of the pit of Halemaumau. What an experience to lay one's self down in peaceful slumber on top of an active volcano.

Mrs. F. B. Campbell, Chicago, Ill., *no date*

We take home many inspiring memories of a very extraordinary trip. We never dreamed that when we awoke this morning the Volcano would be on fire. The sight of the burning fire will not soon be forgotten.

Mary A. Ward, Boston, Mass., 25 July 1929

This is a beautifully calm, clear night. Mauna Loa outlined in moonlight. Rosy glows from volcano tinging cloud clusters underneath the moon. Large fountain in pit very active. Distinct cone formation around secondary fountain. Small active flow on floor of pit into which hardened masses of lava are falling.

Maude B. Thompson, Honolulu, 13 Sept 1934

Meanwhile, visitors continued to be impressed with Dr. Jaggar, the new observatory, and its staff.

Everything was perfect. Our host graciousness itself, and the trip all about the volcano, and the marvelous fern jungle, thanks to the kindness of Dr. Jaggar and Mr. Wingate and Mr. Lamb was even more thrilling and interesting than I had expected.

S. Morgenthau, *no date*

A most interesting and enjoyable visit — thanks to Dr. Jaggar and Mr. Lycurgus.

Franc D. Ingraham, 12 Jan 1938

Back again although no eruption — just came to see Dr. Jaggar.

James H. R. Cromwell, *no date*

Alfred Magoon
Honolulu

Yesterday's trip gave me an entirely new idea of volcanic action. My first impression was of the gentle slope of Mauna Loa, which must mean that the lava is very fluid. Its rapid flow makes a flatter top to the mountain than the more viscous flow characteristic of the volcanic peaks of the Cascade Mountains. The steepness and depth of the craters and the pipes were very striking. I can well understand why this has captured the imagination of Dr. Jaggar and all people of the islands.

Karl T. Compton, M.I.T., Cambridge, Mass.,
21 March 1947

Dr. Finch and Uncle George have made this Park stand out above all others. We can only hope that our return will not be too long.

Dr. and Mrs. Wm. S. Keshadden, *no date*

On May 17, 1955, yesterday, we saw the Puna eruption back in full swing, shooting a steady column of lava 200 feet skyward. According to Dr. Gordon Macdonald, the volcanologist, we were able to get closer to the red lava flow than since the lava flow started on February 28, 1955. The lava fall was only one-half mile from where we watched it and the lava flow itself was about 150 yards.

Mr. and Mrs. John Fraser, residents of the Volcano district, were kind enough to drive us from the Volcano House to the Puna eruption district. And Mr. James Kealoha, chairman of the board of supervisors of Hilo, who was actually superintending the building of new roads over the recent lava flows, led us in his car to the closest spot from which to watch the lava fall, red fountains and lava flow.

A. F. Peters, 18 May 1955

Some things cannot be described; they must be experienced.

Kilauea is wonderful, yet more marvelous is the mind of man that reaches for the solution of the mysteries of the lake of fire and will not be content until there is an abiding appreciation of the greatness of this marvel of Nature, based upon Knowledge.

Thomas Edward Potterton, Brooklyn, New York, 2 Aug 1911

Note: Scattered throughout the Register are many maps drawn by professional surveyors, such as F. S. Dodge and J. M. Lydgate; in fact, some of these maps have been published in other books. However, the emphasis in this book has been to present the writings and drawings of a variety of visitors to the Volcano House, not just the scientists and surveyors; thus most of the drawings in this chapter are the work of amateurs.

Kilauea erupted briefly in 1952 and 1954; an eruption in 1955, on the east rift zone, lasted about three months. At that time, Dr. Gordon Macdonald was director of the Hawaiian Volcano Observatory. One of the last entries in the Volcano House Register describes this eruption.

The last record of volcanic phenomena in the Volcano House Register covers the 1955 eruption of Kilauea. By then the Observatory had been in full operation for decades, monitoring and analyzing volcanic activity, and today it continues the record-keeping that O. H. Gulick initiated in 1865.

Five

PELE, HELLFIRE, AND NIAGARA FALLS

"Nuthin' like it."

MOST VISITORS *to the Volcano House wrote on the same general themes: they gave detailed impressions of Pele, they imagined fiery Halemaumau to be a glimpse of Hell, and they compared Kilauea to Niagara and Vesuvius.*

Visitors wrote a great deal about Pele, the Hawaiian goddess of volcanoes. While some visitors considered Pele a mere superstition, more considered her a real, living goddess to be treated with respect. The varied attitudes toward her are shown in the following selections, which range from light-hearted humor and poetry to serious reverence.

I arrived today and saw the works of this mischievous supernatural being, stilling the fragrant cool uplands closed in with mist, and I kept sniffing the good, pleasant air. There arose in me a great desire, and palpitations of the heart, to do what I had not done before—to view her marvelous works. I turned back as the fog crept along and covered the top of Maunaloa and brought calmness to the "children of Kaluaopele." This is finished; with aloha. [*Translated from Hawaiian.*]

Emalia Kauhane, 27 Nov 1865

E. D. Baldwin
Asst. Gov't. Survey

Visited Madame Pele on the fourteenth and still live.
>Mr. and Mrs. W. Frank Sadd, San Francisco,
>2 Aug 1866

Arrived here eight o'clock this morning from Kapapala. This afternoon, went down to the lake, Madame Pele was sleepy.
>Wm. L. Bond, 1 Oct 1868

Found old Pele rather active during the day, and this evening the old girl is illuminating grandly, but she is not doing her best and as the natives tell us on undoubted authority will not do it again until this present king dies and another is elected. Joe is a good Christian, but he believes in Miss Pele implicitly, giving the reason that it always has been so, even at the recent election of Lunalilo and strange to say argument couldn't convince him against what he has seen.
>A. B. Carter, Lieut., 24 Feb 1873

Christmas eve with naught but Madam Pele's bonfires, a grand sight.
>F. S. Lyman, Hilo, 24 Dec 1880

F. S. Lyman

The Old Woman of the Pit constantly erupts—she does not slacken off her gurgling sounds. [*Translated from Hawaiian.*]
>Jno. N. Kapahu, with wife and Kalele, Naalehu,
>19 Oct 1883

About thirtieth visit—"Same old thing." Everyone who writes in this book seems to think they have been especially favored by Madame Pele.
>C. N. Arnold, Hilo, R. S. Chief Hawaii, 27 April 1884

Not a Fake. For some months it has been my earnest desire to visit the volcano but I was always unfortunate enough to meet people who had visited it, and who when questioned would reply "it is grand" or words to that effect. Their laconic description of the crater made me grow a trifle "leary" as the boys say and visions of a fake crossed my mind when I recalled the man who paid a quarter to see a living mermaid. Of course he was a badly sold man and as he emerged from the tent he was questioned by a large crowd of skeptics who stood outside. He told them that he saw a genuine freak so they paid their money and rushed in. I thought my informants were trying to play the same game on me, but now I can happily say that the Goddess Pele is not a fake but on the contrary I found her to be a very active female.

Charles Rockinghorse, By F.L.H., *no date*

Witnessed the awe-inspiring, fascinating, and incomparable grandeur of Madam Pele's Home.

                              J.J.K., 17 Jan 1910

Arrived at the Crater Hotel at four; left the Hotel and went to see the eruption of The Woman. The eruption of The Woman was beautiful in the dark of night, and I saw the magical works of The Woman of the Pit and I saw Halemaumau and the top of Uwekahuna, so there was much seen. And so I give my deep aloha to the people who live here at this Hotel. The child of Kauai where the sun sinks into Lehua now goes home. With many thanks to Our Father in Heaven, I am in humbleness. [*Translated from Hawaiian.*]

                         Wm. Puaoi, 23 Nov 1910

After centuries of our researches "Pele" illustrates how little we know of the dynamic forces of nature.

                         W.C.G., 16 June 1911

It's a hell of a subject to think out; I'll wait to hear the opinion of Prof. "Vesuvius" Perret before expressing mine; he's now talking it over with Madam Pele—understands the language she speaks—I don't.

              A. P. Taylor, Acting Editor, Advertiser, Honolulu,
              14 July 1911

I am from Arkansas. Now laugh damn you, but this Miss Pele has Arkansas skinned.

                    signature illegible, 14 July 1912

Arrived here at ten minutes to 12 A.M. crater particularly inactive. The presiding Goddess having gone to visit her friend at Mokuaweoweo.
                    Thomas E. Cook, Kealakekua, 26 Aug 1872

Arrived Saturday August 31st. Crater still quiet—it is rumored that Pele has again gone gallivanting off with Kamapuaa.
                    Thomas E. Cook, Kealakekua, 31 Aug 1872

Madame Pele is very capricious and goes and returns without any previous notice. The action is likely to be resumed at any time.
                    H. M. Whitney, 18 May 1896

During periods when Mauna Loa was in eruption and Kilauea quiet, people naturally inferred that Pele had temporarily left her home at Halemaumau to go visiting.

[133]

Some visitors actually addressed Pele herself, presuming that she enjoyed reading the Register.

Aloha to you, Pele, the Chiefly Woman of the Pit. I looked at the bottom of the Pit this morning at nine; there was no fire at this time—only the aa below was to be seen, and the steam. I give my full thanks for the beauty and comfort of this place, the Volcano House. Aloha. [*Translated from Hawaiian.*]

Jesse Peliholani Makainai, Honolulu, 22 Nov 1895

Dear Pele
  I have been visiting you every week since November 1908, and I have never found you as beautiful, and as active as you were in July 1912.

Joe, 10 Dec 1914

Dear Old Pele:
  You surely are some Girl. I will not fail to tell Norwalk, Ohio all about you.

W. C. Whitney, *no date*

They can say what they want about you, Madame Pele, but you are fascinating.

Dorothy Campbell, *no date*

People sometimes made offerings to Pele. Others believed that when offerings were not frequent enough, Madame would occasionally claim one anyway.

The natives seemed less changed than Pele herself, seeing that they still seek to propitiate her by throwing into her supposed den, their shoes, knives, handkerchiefs, and even money, nearly as much as I remember them to have done in days gone by.

Tho. B. Manhauser, schooner yacht Themis, 1 Sept 1865

Three lakes very active. Saw Pele devour an offering given by one of our party.

Anna McCully (second visit), 22–24 May 1872

[134]

After we went down the crater. I lost my hat down the hole, the natives say that Pele came and took it. Certainly there was little wind.
H. Glanville Barnacle and William Yates, Cheshire, England,
20 Dec 1874

Oh, Pele, Pele, goddess of fire,
We do not wish to raise thy ire,
But while we're here
Be of good cheer,
And spurt her up a little higher.
H. G. Woolten, 21 July 1888

Poets have sung of great Pele,
Have praised her and called her most fair;
Raved of her red molten lashes,
And made many rhymes to her hair.
But none have said aught of her loving,
Her lips or her hot eyes that hiss—
Oh, surely the bards worship Pele,
But none of them wants Pele's kiss.
Hayne, 25 Jan 1896

Wonderful things in Nature we see
But none more wonderful Pele than thee.
L. D. Miner, Montreal, Canada, 29 July 1879

Pele's grief is keener and more lasting
    than that of all the widows.
Her lamentations rise unceasingly from
    a pit of woe in Kilauea's heart.
Pele's breath is hot and searing
    as that of a thousand dragons.
Her voice rises in perpetual altercation
    and her tongue's unceasing.

What a shrewish termagant Madame Pele is, and yet how fascinating!
C. H. Michener, 1 June 1912

Many of the poems written in the Register are about Madame Pele.

[135]

To Madame Pele,
Our hats are off to you, fierce queen,
With your hellish smell and your lurid mien
Filling your home with terrors, I ween
Unknown to all and alone by the Devil seen.

Hall, 22 Oct 1916

William W. Hall
Honolulu
Oahu

Visitors to Halemaumau were entranced by Pele and her varied moods.

Madame Pele—You are an old flirt. Your hair is white with age, but your lips are as red, your eyes as fervid, your cheeks as flushed, as in your youth. Goodbye, old dame.

J. Blackman, 13 Aug 1884

We descended into the crater. Pele revealed herself in robes of awful majesty. O Goddess of Hawaiian Lore, enshrouded in the mysteries of eternity, who may know the secrets of thy heart? What scientist may wrest from thy creation or know from whence thou art?

Edward Smith, 9 Aug 1885

Pele never disappoints us—she is wonderful in all of her moods—never twice the same, always fascinating.

Katherine M. Yates, Honolulu, 6 Sept 1912

Madame Pele—truly, a most fascinating dame, warm and glowing in disposition, yet fiery in temper, ruddy of cheek and eyes of dancing flames. Quite the most interesting lady I have yet had the fortune to meet.

George C. Paterson, San Francisco, Calif., 1 Feb 1920

After a week spent with Pele I am still unable to describe her, but I have felt her fascination.

Evelyn Damon Whitman, Oakland, California,
6 April 1921

Our second visit to Pele—first time in February 1924 when she was angry and on rampage, today she is like a lady quiet and refined. Give me Pele in a temper, a sight and thrill you cannot duplicate the world over.
C. A. Webster, Stockton, Calif., 28 Feb 1928

Query: is this, or is it not the place referred to in Scripture, as the "Lake that burneth with fire and brimstone which is the second death." Let those that come after, answer if they can.
Wm. Clark, Honolulu, 18 Aug 1865

Whether or not visitors believed in Pele, the majority did believe in heaven and hell. For most of the years covered by the Volcano House Register, Halemaumau was a lake of molten lava. Many visitors to the volcano, upon seeing this spectacle, were immediately reminded of the final destination of sinners.

The crater seems a slumbering hell ready to belch forth its explosive elements at any time and reminds me of the ancient fabled Grecian legend of the regions of desolation over which the shades of the dead trooped on their journey to the River Styx—there to be rowed across by the old boatman Charon to Hades, the land of ghostly shades. The scene lacking only the silent tideless river to make the resemblance complete.
E. Bieres, Kawatha, Kas., Late Col. 171st Regt.,
17 Feb 1899

I have just returned from the Place that I have read so much about in the Bible, and shall hereafter keep on the right road to Heaven.
Plummette M. Byng, Charleston, S.C., 4 Aug 1885

The most typical response of Halemaumau visitors was to immediately repent of past sins and promise to be good Christians forevermore.

Found Mme. Pele's wrath had been aroused. I thereupon made one of the good resolutions with which Hades is paved.
Mrs. Michael A. Fisher, San Francisco, 9 Dec 1907

On my way up to the volcano, oh how I longed for a wide road—I felt that most any moment my horse would make a mis-step and I'd be hurled down the mountain side. After seeing the wonderful and terrible "Sea of Fire" all thoughts of wide roads were forgotten, hereafter me for the straight and narrow and quiet path.
Mrs. D.W.S., Dallas, Tex., 12 May 1910

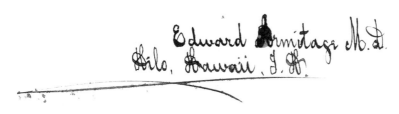

When I first saw the volcano I thought it would make me a better girl, but Dame Fortune was against me.

Maud S. Powell, Reno, Nev., 6 Oct 1910

After viewing this indescribable sight, I am going home and be good all the rest of my life.

W. H. Egerer, Aberdeen, Wash., 18 Jan 1920

Visitors less inclined to repentance simply acknowledged their future home.

With a three foot stick we explored as much of our future residence as we could, but could stir up but little of the fire. It was amusing to see all hands swearing off and renouncing the world, the flesh and the Devil, and vowing to live lives of Christians hereafter.

signature illegible, 19 May 1875

After viewing my future home I have much sympathy for my friends who left before me.

H. Williamson, Denver, Colorado, 14 Sept 1904

It was a rough old trip over here to Hilo—a cussing ride on the train, a worse one on the stage; but at the end of my journey it was Hell. It was well worth the trouble; most everybody likes to take a peep into the future.

Dr. F. E. Frates, San Francisco, 2 Sept 1909

I think that if Mr. Cruzan, instead of preaching sermons, on "A glimpse through an open window into Heaven & Hell" would send his people to the volcano, and see the new lake as it is now, he would do more good.

Alex. Young, Jr., Honolulu, 25 Feb 1886

Some felt that the lake of fire was far more effective than any church sermon.

Halemaumau is the real "Hell" we hear so much of; it tends to make the Sinner repent. Teachers of the Bible should visit Madam Pele often, so as to enable them to deliver their Gospel with great force.

Jno. C. Lane, Honolulu, 9 Sept 1909

One look will do more good than all the ministers in Hawaii.

R.J.S., San Francisco, 31 Dec 1911

Judging from the amount of sulphur and fire do not hesitate to conclude that the devil is at the bottom of it all.

C. S. Rulgnay, 9 March 1903

There were frequent references to the Devil.

We saw his tracks, we smelled his breath. We heard the swish of his tail!

Lura W. Porter, Pasadena, Cal., 10 Dec 1910

Vraiment—c'est la maison du diable!

Neva Broughton, Honolulu, 7 Jan 1921

The "Devil's Throat" and the "Devil's Kitchen." Too much room for the Devil. 'Tis his blandishments that make the place enticing.
Mrs. W. J. Parver, Whittier, Cal., no date

Some visitors decided they wanted to go to Hell, hoping they could thus watch glorious cascades of lava for all eternity.

If hell is like this, that's where I want to go.
Mrs. E. E. Herrscher, San Francisco, Cal., 10 Dec 1920

I never imagined the "Infernal Regions" were so attractive.
Henry A. Wilson, New York City, 20 April 1911

If Hell is anything like this, I don't want to go to Heaven.
signature illegible, 29 Oct 1920

It is like sitting in the front row of heaven watching Hell boil over.
C. A. Hoffman, 20 March 1908

Our first visit to the Volcano and it looks like Hell.
R. J. MacDonald, Butte, Montana, 11 May 1910

I looked today into the fiery crater of Hell, and failed to find a single face of a friend that has gone before me, and am happy.
D. W. Shanks, Dallas, Texas, 12 May 1910

To me the lake has not a suggestion of hell, as so many put it; it is gleaming landscape, veined with gold. Night perfect—conditions ideal—activity intense—an indelible memory, as delightful as lasting.
Frank Newhall White, Chicago, Ill., 3 Aug 1910

After a thorough topographic (and social) reconnaissance of the entrance to Brimstone Bay we have decided to defer the exploration of the interior until we get our Orders.
Paul M. Trueblood, U.S. Coast and Geodetic Survey,
Steamer Explorer, Jan 1911

If anybody is as polite as to tell you go to "Hell," you come to Kilauea.
no signature, 14 Aug 1912

It is without doubt the best place I have ever seen in which to make New Year's Resolutions.

> G. L. Shaffer, San Francisco, Cal., 9 Aug 1915

I never believed in Hell before—nor do I now.

> W. O. Gandy, Chicago, 7 Feb 1915

Better guess again.

When you get ready to shake the dust of this old earth, go to Hawaii, for even at the worst, you must go through Paradise in order to get to hell.

> An Enthusiastic Visitor, 12 March 1920

The most beautiful spot. "A veritable Eden on a potential Hell!"
Anita Rodrick, 25 Dec 1938

Besides comparing Halemaumau to Hell, many visitors compared it to other wonders they had seen, such as Yellowstone, Niagara, and Vesuvius; almost all concluded Kilauea was best. Others compared it to cauldrons of molten iron, 4th of July fireworks, and the "Saline River way down in Arkansaw."

We arrived today at Kilauea; went to see the eruption of the Woman. We did not, however, talk with her. We went, and near to her place we were driven off at all the edges of her supernatural workings because of the intense heat. When we returned here to the guest house it was nearly dark, and shortly afterwards she gave forth her light, and we saw that it was just like the hale mahu of Ulakoheo as it was smelting [*The hale mahu, "steam house," was the Honolulu Iron Works. Translated from Hawaiian.*]
J. Keo, 13 July 1872

"Halemaumau" recalled to one of us, a picturesque lake in New Zealand, only in this case the fluid was of a deep crimson color and showed here and there boiling fountains. A stream of molten lava formed quite a fall divided into two halves by a projecting mass of old lava thus resembling in form the Rainbow Falls Hilo.
H. Wineberg, M. D., Waiohinu, Kau; Edwd. Smith, Deputy Sheriff, Kau, 27 Aug 1881

The Lakes remind me of a boiling cauldron of molten iron as seen in a large retort.
J. H. Burnett, M.E., New York City, 17 Sept 1882

The walk to the South Lake over the crisp lava far easier than a similar experience at Vesuvius. The next day, which was to have been devoted to Kilauea-iki and the neighborhood, we were compelled to spend indoors, no great hardship. The mountain Goddess gave us a taste of her temper and for twenty-four hours poured out the vials of her wrath upon us. I thought I had seen storms on the West Coast of Scotland, but they were tempests in a teacup compared to those initiated by Pele.
Charles Bill, Staffordshire, England, 9–12 Dec 1882

I need only say that it is not even equalled by "Barnum's Greatest Show on Earth."

> A. Hood, Nova Scotia, 25 Dec 1882

It is a startling contrast to the white ashes of the late eruption in New Zealand.

> T. S. Lea, M.A., 24 Feb 1887

The whole scene was most interesting, in our humble opinion, and ranks in the first class of natural wonders, with the Terraces in New Zealand, Yellowstone Park, and many other marvels which it has been our privilege to see.

> Charles G. de Betham, Cambridge, 26 April 1887

Mt. Hood is not in it alongside of Kilauea.

> Ed Dekum, 14 May 1893

Climbed old Haleakala three weeks ago and today saw the crater of Kilauea. After seeing the immense crater of the former, Kilauea looks rather small, but the life and fire in this one lends it an uncanny fascination which the former does not have.

> Mabel A. Thayer, San Rafael, Calif., 29 Oct 1904

Mrs Henry Cockett.

The scenery on the Colombia River is hardly surpassed in the world, and yet we never saw anything so grand in viewing the burning lake in the crater of Kilauea.

> F. N. Gilbert, Portland, Oregon, 26 Feb 1907

If one can imagine a vast omelette of molten lava, some idea of the spectacle may be gathered.

> Ralph G. E. Forster, 4 June 1908

We are fully impressed with the awful grandeur that draws tourists to this natural wonder. I have hitherto thought Crater Lake in the top of Mt. Mazama, the grandest natural phenomenon to be seen, but Halemaumau surpasses everything that I have been privileged to see. There are few sights more terrible and at the same time fascinating.

signature illegible, 24 Sept 1908

The volcano of Kilauea is different from anything I have seen, I can think of nothing it reminds me of, but the fireworks we have at home on the Fourth of July.

Margaret Yandes Bryan, Rochester, N.Y.,
10 March 1909

Halemaumau should be classed as the first and leading wonder of the world. All others sink into insignificance in comparison with it.

A. B. Arleigh, Honolulu, 18 May 1909

H. F. Lewis, Mrs. Lewis, Donald Lewis, Mr. Shingle and Mr. Farrington visited the crater during their tour of the island to witness the water come down at Hamakua when the ditch is opened July 1. Mr. Lewis avers and states on his honor that next to the great irrigation enterprise with which he has been connected the crater of Kilauea is the greatest and most interesting exhibition on earth.

H. F. Lewis, 24 June 1910

Wallace R. Farrington

The volcano is a sight, but honest, the real big sight was to see Miss Putzman on horseback.

C.H.L., 31 July 1910

Looks worse than Pittsburgh and smells like the Reading Railroad.

J.G.R., 21 June 1911

Looking down into the boiling lava, I had to think of the big soap vats in Swifts and Co. Packing Plant in Chicago. The color of the black lava and the motion of things and the smell were somewhat similar. At night the volcano looked like boiling venetian paint in a kettle.

> H. Linde M.D., Cyrus, Minn., 4 Aug 1911

In all our journey we have never seen anything that could compare with it. It far exceeded our greatest imaginations. The glare from this lake of fire reminded us of the great fire of San Francisco April 18, 1906.

> Mr. and Mrs. W. Wallace Dougall, San Francisco, Calif.,
> 25 Feb 1912

Am on my way to the crater. It is the greatest thing I ever saw but not as great as the old Saline river way down in Arkansaw.

> C. B. Murphy, Haskell, Ark., 1912

Connecticut has no volcano to equal Kilauea!

> Mrs. A. Kelsey, Meridin, 8 March 1915

You ought to visit "our house" on Saturday night when my old man comes home, the Volcano ain't a candle compared to it.

> Peter Burke, 26 April 1918

Nuthin' like it in Oklahoma.

> H. T. Collins, 8 April 1920

We have nothing like this in California! Truly wonderful.

> Mrs. Elmer B. Burns, Santa Ana, California,
> 18 April 1920

Very well done, the only thing we haven't got in New York.

> Eldiva Brown, N.Y.C., 22 April 1920

I used to think the Grand Canyon of the Colorado was the most wonderful sight but now I know Halemaumau surely surpasses it.

> Katherine Faulkner, Los Angeles, Calif., 12 July 1920

Grand as they are, our Taal and Mayan volcanoes cannot compare with the view enjoyed from this Volcano House.

> M. Saverra, Manila, Phil. Islands, 22 Aug 1920

Have seen the glaciers of the Northland—but Kilauea stands in a class by itself.

> Adele Le Loude Bunting, Skagway, Alaska,
> 4 April 1921

Talk about Brazil being hot. Bet you that 'alemaumau Pit is ten times worse.

> Ed. de Azuiar d'Amrade, S. Paulo, Brazil, 18 July 1921

Compared to Solfatara, the luxury of the foliage & bloom makes this a vision of Paradise.

> Edwin Sommerich, N.Y., 6 March 1930

> I come from Bonnie Scotland
> Whose heather hills are grand
> But Oh, they can't compete
> With this Volcano land.
> A. Archibald, 19 June 1935

Loads better than Schofield Barracks.

> Edith Rutledge, 22 June 1937

Six

EDITOR'S CHOICE

"Words fail me."

BETWEEN THE YEARS *1865 and 1955, Halemaumau was more often than not a molten lava lake. Visitors were awe-struck by the sight. The majority who wrote in the Register seem to have agreed that it was impossible to do justice to the crater with mere words. Yet most writers still felt that if they could string enough adjectives together, they could convey to others a sense of the grandeur they had witnessed.*

It is a sight never to be forgotten, and to be appreciated it must be seen. I believe that no description ever has or ever will be written however comprehensive that can convey anything more than the most vague conception of this wonderful and mysterious creation of the great Creator.

B. F. Dillingham, 4 Sept 1874

I came, I saw, and was astonished.

D. B. Griffin, 9 Dec 1872

The sublimity and awfulness of the scene I leave for others to describe.
H. Deacon, Waiakea, first visit, 23 March 1880

Had a grand view of the burning lake which was the grandest sight I ever saw in my life. The sight was perfectly grand beyond description. The grand scenery which is beyond human description will ever remind me of the grand lesson we read about in the Bible but seeing is believing and after having seen the grand sight I feel grand beyond everything and advise everybody who can possibly do so to visit this one of the grandest things not to be seen in this world outside of this.

Simon Cohen, London, 24 Feb 1883

It is useless to try and describe what we saw. I will only say that the scene was complete in its terrible grandeur.

Theo H. Davies and family, 10 Aug 1883

Occasionally, a visitor would have a more down-to-earth appraisal.

Left Hilo yesterday morning and after a nine hour ride reached this place. Next day visited the wonders of nature which was satisfactory.

John B. Meldrum, Provo City, Utah, 8 Feb 1884

Rhoda Green Thayer (5th visit)
Nack Warren Thayer, (8th visit)

But such an opinion was rare among the claims of "grand" and "sublime."

Grand beyond description.

G. Bertram, 10 March 1884

I was simply electrified by what I saw, the sublimity and grandeur of the scene should really be described by those who possess the element of poetry in their soul and who are capable of expressing themselves properly.

Adolph Mack, San Francisco, 17 March 1884

Found the new lake quite active and regretted to turn our backs to so grand a sight. It beggars description, and I will not here attempt any flights of poetical prose, for they will be sure not to reach the first ridge of the summit of description it demands. It surpassed my most imaginative conception, and the awful and silent surroundings give to the fires of Hell a deeper and direr aspect.

Geo. Bixby, Long Beach, California, 28 Sept 1887

There are numerous other points of fountain-play which sometimes work in concert. At such times the display is magnificent. This it is that makes the sightseer stagger with the weight of big words.

N. B. Emerson, 18 Aug 1908

[148]

All the sentiments and words of praise and admiration thus far written in this book, are but a faint echo of the profound impression a studious view of the volcano forces upon the observer. To the casual on-looker, even to the unthinking one, must come a sense of the awful sublimity of these volcanic wonders; and it is fitting here to remark that I have taken the utmost, the highest degrees in the order of the unthinkers.

S. A. Raphael, San Francisco, Cal., 2 June 1893

It is absolutely indescribable.

George Smith, Buffalo, N.Y., 18 Nov 1893

Have just returned from a trip to the crater of Kilauea. No pen picture nor word portraiture can adequately convey to the human mind, the faintest conception of this awfully grand and terrible work of nature's action.

J. Lewis Crew, Philadelphia, 26 Sept 1901

It would be an idle and futile task for one to portray the awful and majestic grandeur of the seemingly bottomless chasm of Halemaumau.

E. A. Douthitt, 26 Jan 1903

I am at a loss of words to express the grandeur.

Mae R. Weir, Honolulu, 30 Oct 1905

The fierce grandeur of it all defies expression by pen or language in any manner. The pen of scribe, brush of artist, or language of the most eloquent orator, are all absolutely inadequate.

Dr. Erasmus W. Carson, Cataline Island, Calif.,
13 March 1907

I had heard many descriptions of the crater in activity but without being an eye-witness, I hardly see how it is possible for any one to get a true idea of its grandeur.

Molly Alatau Wilder, 2 April 1908

KILAUEA IN ACTION 1908.

It is a grand and awesome sight, never to be forgotten.

Emily A. Baldwin, Puunene, Maui, 17 Nov 1908

It is simply impossible to exaggerate in words the grandeur of the volcano of Kilauea to people who have never seen it.

D. G. May, 4 June 1908

Wonderful beyond belief.

Chas. J. Biart, Honolulu, 17 June 1908

No use trying. Words are empty.

W. H. Bliss, 25 June 1908

It is useless to try to describe the indescribable! No words or description can give the slightest idea of the marvellous and unspeakable glories of Kilauea Crater—unique in the whole world.

no signature, 11 March 1909

You've got to see it—adjectives don't describe it so that another could get any idea of what an unusual awe inspiring spectacle it really is.

Henry McIntyre, San Diego, California, 18 March 1909

Mrs. G. K. Wilder

[151]

Could we transfer our feelings on paper, there would be no space for those guests who are to follow. There is no doubt but that Halemaumau is the most stupendous, awe inspiring sight nature has produced.

Mrs. G. V. Rogers, 22 May 1909

I found the volcano indescribable.

Catherine Magoon, 14 Aug 1909

This is the first time I ever visited the volcano, and just let me tell the public that words cannot explain how wonderful it is, why there is nothing that I know of that can compare with it.

Mrs. B. C. Kennedy, San Francisco, 8 Jan 1910

Grand and sublime is the only way I can describe my thoughts as I viewed this picture of God's handiwork, a sight of which I know no equal.

Mrs. Hattie Pollard Barnum, *no date*

Wonder of wonders. Indescribable.

Ramona Marks, *no date*

Kilauea is simply beyond description. I give it up even before I start.

A. C. MacNeil, Chicago, 5 Oct 1910

It is certainly most wonderful! There are no words to express it.

Mary R. Prince, Saint Paul, Minn., 15–17 Feb 1911

The most magnificent and awe inspiring sight I have ever seen.

F. F. Lippett, Petaluma, California, 20 April 1911

A wonderful sight. No limit. No measure. Unfathomable. Impossible.

P. W. Rider, Kakaako Mission, Honolulu, 15 June 1911

Beyond description.

Allan J. W. Keeler, Los Angeles, Calif., 14 July 1911

Words fail me!

Lucy A. Harbison, *no date*

Awful in the true meaning of the word, that is, awe inspiring.
W. D. Peach, Schofield Barracks, H.T., 8 Jan 1915

An indescribable sight never to be forgotten.
Mr. and Mrs. Walter G. Vodden, San Francisco, Calif.,
18 Jan 1915

There aren't adjectives enough in the Dictionary to describe this magnificent sight.

Augusta C. Glass, *no date*

All these men visited the volcano, and none can describe its wonder.
Roy B. Loveless, 12 Sept 1917

I am powerless to describe it.
Roderick N. Matson, Cheyenne, Wyoming, 3 Jan 1918

The one thing here most indescribable beyond all I've seen, yea even the flow of lava, is this everlasting flow of beautiful, flowery, and lurid, sulphurous language.

no signature, 10 Feb 1920

Indescribable.

Flora Henzel, New York City, 6 June 1920

Mere words cannot express its beauty and awfulness.
Helen E. Noble, Los Altos, California, 10 July 1920

There is nothing can be said that would express my idea of this truly wonderful spectacle.

E. A. Schiller, Atlanta, Ga., 19 Feb 1921

[153]

Words cannot describe its awe inspiring grandeur.

George O. Connor, Chicago, 23 Dec 1921

Stupendous, alluring and indescribable.

Mr. & Mrs. Chas. A. Frantz, *no date*

Speechless!

signature illegible, 7 Dec 1929

One feels the great insignificance in the face of such a powerful destructive force, and the word "awful" really means something.

Mrs. Parker M. Paine, *no date*

Beyond description.

Mrs. Chas B. Cordary, California, 21 Oct 1931

As the preceding entries demonstrate, much of the material in the Volcano House Register is repetitious. Some visitors couldn't think of anything to write, so they copied the preceding entries, even to the point of plagiarizing. Other entries contain original thoughts or splendid descriptions. Here are some of the more vivid entries describing the molten lava lake.

We walked four or five miles over fields of lava where the flow had assumed fantastic shapes, sometimes twisted together like coils of rope and sometimes heaped up in petrified fountains. Reaching the lake, we found it surrounded by banks one hundred and fifty feet high, and ringed around the edge with a line of liquid lava that kept bubbling and boiling upward in glowing cascades.

L.M.C., 17 March 1874

Arrived at the Volcano House August 20 at 3 P.M. Kilauea and Halemaumau very little active but the new crater, Kilauea Keki, rose short time after my arrival and gave me a grandiose size. Remained there till dark and watched very eagerly every motion, noticed that the Kilauea Keki increase her flood and ran rapidly down to the old lake of the Kilauea, both mingled together, about a dozent bubles appeared and the whole was an ocean of fire, with hundreds of little craters. Visited afterward the different funnels of sulphur and steam. Had a very long walk home to the vulcano house, arrived there 9:15 P.M., fine supper.

August 21. Had a beautiful sleep, but as it was very cold this morning we had a little fire in the parlor, what a difference to Honolulu. Visited today the sulphur baths and openings, and started again for the field of action at 5 P.M. Would advise every ladie and gentleman to visit the craters at night or evening after dark, at daylight no one would get the real im-

Dec. 9th 1874

Lilia K. Dominis.
S. Kipi
Annie B. Aldrich.
Mary Ann Buke
Evelyne M. Wilson
Nikoa Kipi
O P Holt
George H Holt
Hannah Holt

pression of an active vulcano as it is at night time. The guide is Kapuniai,
very good and true, as a patience to return at night.

> Heinrich Berger, commanded as Bandmaster for the
> Royal Hawaiian Troops, 21 Aug 1875

When the last ray of sunlight had disappeared behind the summit of
Mauna Loa, the Goddess Pele introduced a grand pyrotechnic display
for our entertainment. Clouds of smoke hanging over Halemaumau and
the new crater were illuminated by the glowing fire beneath, and exhibited every shade of light from a burning vermillion to the palest red as
the seething mass below varied in the intensity of its brilliancy. And
beneath this overhanging curtain, the playful Goddess was toying with
the liquid fire, tossing up great handfuls and scattering it about in showers
of fiery spray. Small patches of evanescent flame would dart upward and
burn brilliantly for a few moments, and then slowly dying out, would be
succeeded by others equally beautiful, brought forth like their predeces-
sors to live the same short but "shining" life. Every new outburst and

every varying shade of light seemed to possess fresh charms, and at a late hour, even after our long ride, we were loth to leave the verandah and retire for the night.

George W. Stewart, California, 20 Aug 1881

The afternoon proved very inclement and a cold rain fog drifting from the snows of Mauna Kea enveloped the landscape and held us in unwilling bondage until bedtime. Then there was a sudden transfiguration. The fog-mist rolled away and the eternal fires of Halemaumau painted themselves in lurid colours on the retreating clouds. Words are wanting to do justice to the awe-inspiring scene. The black, frowning, and altogether forbidding cliffs tinged with a Hellish glare. The black floor—across which fiery serpents seemed to writhe in agony. Fountains of liquid fire flung white hot jets of lava into the sulphurous air whose recoiling billows flung themselves in vain against the enclosing rocks. These and a hundred other manifestations of power created a scene of devilish horror that no time can obliterate or soften.

M.J.C., Queensland, Australia, 30–31 May 1883

Visited the Lakes of Fire and found them beautiful beyond all descriptions we had ever read—fire fountains, Atlantic waves, fiery serpents, golden ice—no words can tell the ever-changing glories of the molten lava! The island in the New Lake resembled the Rock of Gibraltar—with the lights of the town beneath, and this was surrounded by a sea of gold splashing in waves, and circling with a view of brilliant light the margin of the lake.

Major and Mrs. Carr Dyer, England, 27 June 1884

We have looked upon the purple floor and watched the seams of yellow and crimson stretch out and open, a fringe upon the wrinkled purple. Again we have watched the river of gold surge through dark caves and as it circled, draw in a blackened mass, converting it into its own bright substance. Best of all to see a sudden concentration of circles and then a splashing upwards—a fountain of liquid fire, scattering its newly coined mintings far and wide.

Mrs. M. P. Benton, 29 July 1887

Kilauea with its lava lapping the sides of the basin is like the ocean ever reaching for something to devour, ever changing—at times resembling

STARTING FOR AND RETURNING FROM THE VOLCANO.

a beautiful golden sunset, then its jagged streaks like lightning and the roaring is like the thunder. One feels the power of our maker. Words can never describe it—it is the sight of a lifetime.

no signature, no date

The most beautiful feature of the display was the cascade of fire issuing from the cone. This cascade was ever changing. It spread out, fell back, burst into millions of glowing stars, dotting the floor below like a tropic sky on a cloudless night. Your imagination swept you from this realm of mortals and placed you side by side with the Creator as he built the heavens and the stars. Worlds were in the making and transported back through eons of time you saw it all just as it occurred.

C. N. Towne, Mapimi, Mexico, 21 March 1908

Halemaumau was overwhelmingly impressive, leaving most visitors completely amazed and barely able to contain themselves as they expressed their feelings. Yet occasional writers noted the need to look at the other beauties of nature in the area as well, and to do so slowly, quietly, and sensitively.

As one member of our little party has alluded to some of the greater points connected with a visit to this wonderful place it may not be out of place to note some smaller items. If you live at a distance you will probably never come here again. So don't be in too much of a hurry. There is some responsibility coupled with this one opportunity. Many have lived and died without this sight and many more who would gladly have the privilege will never realize it.

Go to the sulphur banks—hear the steam ooze out through the sulphur cones—see the exquisitely delicate feathery crystals like yellow frost on the summit margins of the cones.

Sit down on these bluffs in front of the house early in the morning or in the evening and listen to some very sweet warblers that sing free. Don't let some one be talking to you all the time but let all the surroundings have their full effect on you and with the flowers and ferns and birds around you, and the bleak-walled black-floored chasm before you, there comes a grand sense of *loneness* which is not *lonesomeness*.

Joseph Moore, Richmond, Indiana, 2 Feb 1875

James Walter A. H.

The pahoehoe, at first sight so monstrous and unattractive, soon becomes interesting masses of blackened ropes, twisted and coiled; the gentle ripples of the ocean, hardened into black stone; or hillocks of tangled tree trunks, seared and blackened—fantastic forms everywhere.

To best appreciate the splendor of the scene, one needs to leave it for a time, walk about to gather masses of Pele's hair or fantastic bits of lava, then return when the darkness of night has settled about the fathomless pit. Lurid lights playing upon the walls of the awful abyss, the increased glare of the crimson waves, the brightness of the scintillating sparks, the gloriously lighted heavens—all add to the splendor of the scene.

Minnie L. Mackay, Santa Clara, California, 13 Aug 1908

Arrived yesterday coming on foot from Glenwood in two hours. The tramp is well worth making. Strange flowers abound along the road and delicious berries offer agreeable refreshment. A wealth of roses breathes a scented welcome and the red bird keeping company through the lehuas with the scarlet butterfly, seem to vie with each other in pleasing the ear and eye of the wayfarer. The pit of Kilauea is one of the milestones of creation and Halemaumau's fires a caustic commentary on man's estimate of time, space, and himself. The Volcano House would alone be worth a visit. In the garden bloom California poppies and the largest and sweetest violets I have ever seen. What cheer there is of an evening in the smoking-room with its log fire and lounges, every line of which spell comfort. How good it seems after a residence in a tropic town to turn in under the eider-down needed to protect from the cold. Pele's power and Host Demosthenes' rare hospitality have woven a spell around me which the years will not break and which will surely draw me back here again.

Herbert Melton Ayres, 5 Jan 1909

[159]

We came to view Kilauea, and having seen, are satisfied. It is awe-inspiring. For two days we waited for the liquid sunshine to become less liquid, and the third day it was glorious. Having the whole day before us we wandered slowly over the great lava fields and from every point of view watched Kilauea and Halemaumau in all her moods. As night came on we sat gazing almost spellbound at the ever changing lake of fire. As darkness gathered, small red stars appeared in the grey lava, and as the stars were twinkling in the Heavens showing us great snow-crowned Mauna Loa, we had cold white stars above us and red hot stars beneath us. Ever changing—All absorbing lake of fire. We will carry away with us a vivid memory of your glories.

Mr. and Mrs. E. G. Crawford, Vancouver, Wash.,
4 Feb 1911

The skies are blue. The day sparkles. I have rambled on mossy pathways, in the cool, green sanctity of the woods, where little pink roses smiled their welcome; and ginger blossoms, poised on their stalks like groups of pale butterflies, wafted me their tropic sweetness. The trail is fringed with graceful ferns, their tender new leaves as curly and pink as a new-born baby's toes. Here and there among the ferns rise thinly billowing clouds of steam—and in one of the clouds, I saw a rainbow.

In and out among the soft, dull green of lehua foliage, flashed bright glints of color, as tiny scarlet birdlets sought the sister-scarlet of the tasseled blossoms—and as they sought, they made the morning joyful with their simple, happy little songs.

As I walked on, surrounded by all this loveliness, the thought was strong within me: God has done his share. Should we not strive to the utmost to make the human side of the world as beautiful?

signature illegible, no date

Mark Twain wrote in the Register; the original page was removed, but a newspaper article reprinted his words.

Like others who came before me, I arrived here. I traveled the same way I came: most of the way. But I know there was a protecting Providence over us all, and I felt no fear. We have had a good deal of weather. Some of it was only so-so (and to be candid the remainder was similar.) But, however, details of one's trifling experiences during his journey hither may not always be in good taste in a book designed as a record of volcanic phenomena, therefore let us change to the proper subject. We visited the crater intending to stay all night, but the bottle containing our provisions got broke, and we were obliged to return. But while we were standing near the South Lake, 250 yards distant, we saw a lump of dirt about the size of a piece of chalk. I said: 'In a moment there is something unusual going to happen.' We stood by for a sure, and waited, but nothing happened—not at that time. But soon afterward we observed another cloud of dirt about the same size. It hesitated, shook and then fell into the lake. Oh, God! It was awful! We then took a drink. Few visitors will ever achieve the happiness of having two such experiences as the above in succession. While we lay there, a puff of gas came along and we jumped up and galloped over the rough lava in the most ridiculous manner, leaving our blankets behind. We did it because it was fashionable and because it makes one appear to have had a thrilling adventure. We then took another drink after which we returned and camped a little closer to the lake. I mused and said "How the stupendous grandeur of this magnificently terrible and sublime manifestation of celestial power doth fill the poetic soul with grand thoughts and grander images, and how the overpowering solemnity. . ." Here the gin gave out. In the careless hands of Brown, the bottle broke.

Mark Twain, 7 June 1866

I went to Bird Park but did not see a bird. I looked for a Kona nightingale & saw one at last much to my disappointment.

Vera J. Chang, Honolulu, 11 Aug 1936

> At first I thought
> These islets in the sea
> Were crumbs of bliss let down from Heaven
> But now of lava wrought
> I see
> They're loaves from out the devil's oven.

O. P. Nichols, 22 Oct 1882

A good wind this day—
"The smoke of the pit rises straight up
And also that of Mokuaweoweo"

[Translated from Hawaiian. From a mele, not necessarily that Mokuaweoweo was also steaming that day]

Jno. N. Kapahu, 5 May 1884

One of the most amusing entries in the Register is that of a would-be bird-watcher who discovered the hard way that donkeys in Hawaii have a special nickname.

Most poetry in the Register is flowery, corny, lacking in meter and downright dreadful. But occasionally, poems are quite witty and clever.

After a long, a rugged and a rainy ride
How pleasant to sit down by a bright fireside!
With a cheery glimmer and a warming glow
Like the hearth that welcomed us long ago
The fires of Kilauea may never return
But long as their memory ever shall burn
In the mind of this straggler who has seen but their embers
(If naught else of Pele he remembers)
A radiant reminiscence ever shall dwell
Of the good cheer found at the Volcano Hotel.
> Daniel Logan, Editor, Daily Bulletin, 23 March 1886

To me
Tis not Hell
But Nature most sublime.
> C. A. Warner, Los Angeles, Calif., 6 Nov 1893

The "suggestion," the "grandeur," as all men will find,
Is like many other things—all in the mind;
Drop off your adjectives, write the facts, all
And "Old Kilauea" gets most blooming small.
> I.S.A.W., 22 Jan 1896

There is a town not far from here, whose fame is far widespread
Of all wet places on this earth, it stands right at the head.
There is no need to say to you that it is great Hilo.
Not long ago I went down there to spend a week or so.
'Twas raining when I reached there, and if you want to bet,
I'll wager money, love, or chalk, that it is raining yet.
The rain came down in torrents, it drenched me through and through
The people laughed at me and said, Why this is only dew.
They just remove their shoes and hose and let their Trilbies air
The harder that the rain comes down, the less they seem to care.
A friend of mine came round for me to take a walk with him
I said you must excuse me but I never learned to swim
A slicker place than this said he you'll never find again
Said I they wear the slickers to keep away the rain.
Another thing that I don't like, your liquors are too high
And though I'm wet most all the time, most all the time I'm dry.

But now it's time to say adieu, for I must get away
If you ever come to Frisco, just call on F.A.J.

F.A.J., 15 Aug 1896

> To see eternal fires burn
> Two routes there are—alack!
> To view one you must die—the other;
> Five dollars there and back.
>
> Both places are about the same
> But with this difference—well,
> You can come back from Kilauea
> But you can't return from Hell.
>
> Heaven or Hades, when I die,
> I have no choice, I think;
> If things are run there same as here
> With Lycurgus at the brink.

C. F. Merrill, 9 June 1912

These tributes to the Volcano are true I presume,
But all we saw was sulphur fumes.

Mrs. Anna Hutton, Pasadena, California, 22 May 1913

> Aloha Madame Pele
> May your fires never cease
> Demosthenes stays by you
> Tho' his heart's away in Greece.

Pop, 11 July 1913

The curfew tolls the knell of parting day
But somehow I don't want to go away
Far from the madding crowds' ignoble strife
I'd rather pass the remnant of my life

Although to-day the Teuton with his wiles
Capitulated—and the whole world smiles
Still haunts my heart one sweetly solemn strain
'Tis this—"When chance affords I'll come again."

Robert Navarre Corbaley, 11 Nov 1918

The Start for the
FERN FOREST
January 24 1917

[163]

THE ISLAND OF HAWAII

If you could see Hawaii as it past appeared to me
Great Big Lazy Islands spouting from a tropic sea
Dotted with big plantations, each with village and with mills
And the town of Hilo nestling just below its sloping hills
Its two great snow capped mountains stand as sentinels to guard
A lake of red hot lava which is spread in their front yard
No brush can paint its beauties, no pen half its glories tell
It's just a glimpse of heaven with a little dash of hell.

"Daddy" J. B. Silverwood, 30 April 1920

HAWAII

Sand dunes that bark at you
Flowers that bloom by night
Fish that fly
Rainbows at midnight
A Devil's Throat
Tropical snows
Liquid sunshine
Kanaka moon
Golf on the brink of a volcano.

no signature, no date

Often, a single line or a short paragraph expresses a thought more clearly than pages of writing could.

Heaven and hell appear to touch each other.

signature illegible, 9 Nov 1879

We have looked upon the crimson sea.

Wm. H. Woodwell, 19 April 1882

Great is the climb up to the Crater—great our pleasure in going down to the pit, great the blazing of the lava—there are many orange-petaled huapala [sweetheart vine flowers] along the way to reach the crater from Keauhou. [*Translated from Hawaiian.*]

Kaululuimalama, Kula Lahua, Honolulu, 4 Aug 1885

As for the object of our journey, the volcano, I say nothing. The sentimental may gush and the scientific may speculate, but there are things in this world of ours which are so far beyond any expression of emotion or even the comprehension of human knowledge that we simply wish to bow

Christmass 1909

This is Fritz

Post cards burned in the red hot lava cracks. Kilauea.

THE HAIR-RAISING ASCENT OF
THE SIDE OF **KILAUEA IKI** BY
THREE VALIANT YOUTHS FROM
THE VOLCANO HOUSE ON THE
SEVENTH DAY OF JULY, 1902

before them in reverence, and acknowledge the Infinite who created them. The volcano of Kilauea is one of them and we have no desire to belittle it by description or explanation.

J. B. McChesney, Oakland, Cal., 17 June 1886

It is a fairy tale.

Allen J. Black, *no date*

There is a fascination about the scene which must be felt, since it cannot be described.

E. L. Bingham, Reno, Nevada, 26 Dec 1906

"We look before and after, and pine for what is not."
"Our sincerest laughter with some pain is fraught."

But this is one of the times — the rare times — when one is entirely content to live in the present alone.

W. R. Bittenger, 2 March 1907

The floor of the lake presented the appearance of fiery lacery.

J. R. McLaughlin, Seattle, Wa., 27 March 1908

The longer one looks, the more he feels its awful power. It fascinates, enthralls, overwhelms. It beggars description, for no tongue however gifted, no pen however facile, no brush however skillful can picture Halemaumau. The camera cannot measure its depths, convey its sounds, or depict its glow. Those and only those who have looked into its depths, heard its roar or felt its burning heat can ever know the power, the wonder, the magic of the spell it casts upon one.

Frances King Headler, Los Angeles, 11 June 1909

The contrasts of creation — snow-kissed Mauna Kea — firefurnaced Kilauea.

J. L. Hopwood, 28 Aug 1909

A lake of golden fountains.

Elizabeth Weed Shutes, 1 Sept 1910

Gathered many weeds and pleasant memories around Kilauea.
Joseph F. Rock, Botanist, 13 April 1911

Having been married for forty-four years and having been so surrounded by wife, children and grandchildren that I could not stray across a potato patch, I have fallen to the wiles of your siren volcano and should like to lay my bones at her side.
F. B. Wilder, Los Angeles, Calif., *no date*

Wherever I am, I'll never forget that wondrous sight. Thousands of little waves of gold lava and fountains of dazzling fire drops.
Gertrude Thomas, Piedmont, California, 27 April 1912

Beyond even an attempt at explanation of its magic.
Stanley Harker, Los Angeles, Calif., 28 Oct 1917

The most extravagant statement I have ever read or heard concerning it is not overdrawn.
James C. McLaughlin, Muskegon, Michigan,
13 Nov 1917

There are sights in this world that words are useless to describe.
Bernice Kahanamoku, Honolulu, T.H., 10 Sept 1918

I stood on the brink midst the darkness and the stars, and watched o'er come by the wonder of it all.
Pearl Camblin, Los Angeles, California, 7 April 1919

A tropic sunset veiled in clouds of vapor and of smoke,
A school of flaming dragons in a sea of molten gold.
R. V. Sternbergh, *no date*

I have come. I have seen. I have been captivated by the grandeur of this mountain.

signature illegible, no date

In this fascinating place between Heaven and Hell—there is a temptation to linger in Purgatory and rest a while.
Merlon Francis Green, 6 Dec 1949